THE WORLD'S GREATEST MILITARY SPIES AND SECRET SERVICE AGENTS

THE WORLD'S GREATEST MILITARY SPIES AND SECRET SERVICE AGENTS

GEORGE BARTON

Srishti
PUBLISHERS & DISTRIBUTORS

Srishti Publishers & Distributors
A unit of AJR Publishing LLP
212A, Peacock Lane
Shahpur Jat, New Delhi – 110 049
editorial@srishtipublishers.com

First published by
Srishti Publishers & Distributors in 2021

Contents

1

Bell Boyd: The confederate girl who saved Confederate Jackson

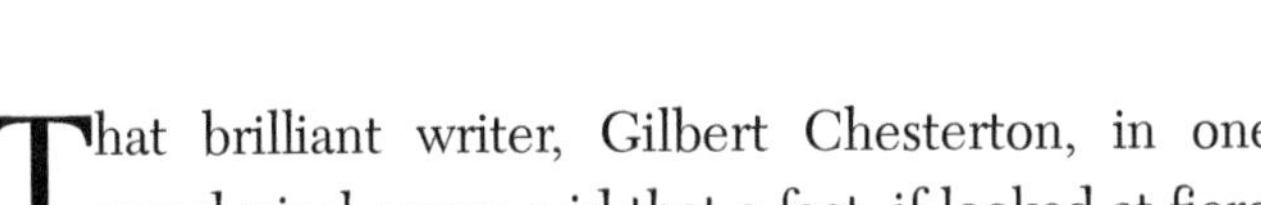

That brilliant writer, Gilbert Chesterton, in one of his paradoxical essays said that a fact, if looked at fiercely, may become an adventure. It is certain that the most important facts in the life of Belle Boyd, the Confederate spy, constitute some of the most thrilling adventures in the great conflict between the sections – the Civil War in the United States.

She was only a girl when the flag was fired on at Sumter and her father and all the members of her family immediately enlisted in the Confederate army. When the Union troops took possession of Martinsburg, Belle Boyd found herself unwillingly inside the Federal lines. She had no formal commission from any of the Southern officers, but circumstances and her ardent nature made her an intense partisan of what was to be "The Lost Cause."

During the occupation of Martinsburg, she shot a Union soldier, who, she claimed, had insulted a Southern woman. From that moment until the close of the war she was actively engaged either as a spy, a scout or an emissary of the Confederacy. On more than one occasion she attracted the attention of Secretary of War Stanton, and although she served a term in a military prison, she seems to have been treated with unusual leniency. After the war she escaped to England, where she published her autobiography, bitterly assailing the victorious North.

It was in Martinsburg that Belle Boyd first began her work for the Confederacy. The Union officers sometimes left their swords and pistols about the houses which they occupied, and later were surprised and mystified at the strange disappearance of the weapons. They little thought that this mere slip of a girl was the culprit. Still later they were amazed to find that these same swords and pistols had found their way into the hands of the enemy and were being used against them.

But aside from this Belle Boyd made it her business to pick up all the information that was possible concerning the movements and the plans of the Union forces. Every scrap of news she obtained was promptly conveyed to General J.E.B. Stuart and other Confederate officers.

BELLE BOYD

It was about the time of the battle of Bull Run that the Confederate general in command fixed upon Front Royal as a site for a military hospital. Belle Boyd was one of the nurses and many a fevered brow felt the touch of her cool hand and more than one stricken soldier afterwards testified to the loving care he received from this remarkable woman.

Later, Front Royal became the prize of the Union army, and Belle Boyd naturally fell under suspicion. Some remarks of her activities had already reached the front, and the officers kept her under close scrutiny. Fortunately, as she thought, she had been provided with a pass which would permit her to leave the place. Accordingly, the second day after the arrival of the Unionists she packed her grip and prepared to leave the town. As she came from the house she was halted by a Union officer named Captain Bannon.

"Is this Miss Belle Boyd?"

"Yes."

"Well, I am the Assistant Provost Marshal, and I regret to say that orders have been issued for your detention. It is my duty to inform you that you cannot proceed until your case has been investigated."

This did not suit the young woman at all. She opened her pocketbook and produced a bit of pasteboard.

"I have here a pass from General Shields. Surely that should be sufficient to permit me to leave the city."

The young officer was perplexed. He did not care to repudiate a pass issued by General Shields, and at the same time did not wish to disobey the instructions which he had received from his immediate chief.

"I hardly know what to do," he said. "However, I am going to Baltimore with a squad of men in the morning. I will take you with me and when we get there turn you over to General Dix."

This program was carried out and the Confederate spy was given a free trip to the monumental city, which she did not want. She was compelled to remain in Baltimore for some time, being kept constantly under the closest supervision. Finally, however, General Dix gave her permission to return to her home. There was no direct evidence against her and it was considered a waste of time and energy to keep her under guard. She was escorted to the boundaries of her old home by two Union soldiers. It was twilight when she arrived at the Shenandoah River. The effects of the war were to be seen on every side. The bridges had been destroyed, and they only managed to cross the river by means of a temporary ferry boat that had been pressed into service.

When she reached her home she found that it had been appropriated as a headquarters by General Shields and the members of his staff. He treated her courteously and said that no harm would befall her if she was discreet and attended to her own business. She was told that a small house adjoining the family dwelling had been set aside for her use, and that the soldiers would be given orders not to molest her in any way.

But the young daughter of the Confederacy kept her eyes and ears open and the night before the departure of General Shields, who was to give battle to General Jackson, she learned that a council of war was to be held in the drawing-room of the Boyd home. Just over this apartment was a bedroom containing a large closet. On the night of the council she managed to make her way to this room and slipped into the closet. A hole had been bored through the floor, whether by design or otherwise she was unable to tell. However, she immediately determined to take advantage of what she considered a providential situation.

When the council assembled the girl got down on her hands and knees in the bottom of the closet and placed her ear near the hole in the floor. To her great satisfaction she found that she could distinctly hear all of the conversation. The conference between the Union officers lasted for hours, but she remained motionless and silent until it had been concluded. When the scraping movement of the chairs on the floor below was heard she knew that everything was over so came out of her place of concealment. She was tired and her limbs were so stiff from remaining in that cramped position so long that it was all she could do to move. But she was full of grit and determination and as soon as the coast was clear she hurried across the courtyard and made the best of her way to her own room in the little house and wrote down in cipher – a cipher of her own – everything of importance that she had overheard.

After that it was but a matter of a few minutes to decide on her course of action. She knew that it would be extremely dangerous to call a servant or to do anything that might arouse the officers, who had by this time gone to bed, so she went to the stables and saddled a horse herself, and galloped away in the direction of the mountains. The moon was shining when she started on this wild ride. She had in her possession passes which she had obtained from time to time for Confederate soldiers who were returning south. Without them it would have been impossible for her to have accomplished her purpose. Before she had gone a half mile she was halted by a Federal sentry. He grabbed the bridle of her horse and cried out:

"Where are you going?"

"I am going to visit a sick friend," was the ready response.

"You can't do it," he cried. "You ought to know that you can't leave this place without a pass."

"But I have one," she said, with an engaging smile, and drew out the piece of pasteboard.

The guard looked at it dubiously, but it was in proper form and contained the necessary signature and he grudgingly permitted her to continue on her journey.

Twice again she was halted by sentinels and each time she told the same story and underwent the same experience. Once clear of the chain of sentries she whipped her horse and hurried ahead for a distance of fifteen miles. At that time the animal was in a perfect lather and when she pulled up in front of the frame house which was the dwelling place of her friends the horse was panting and trembling from the unusual exertion. She leaped from the animal's back and going to the door rapped on it with the butt end of her riding whip. There was no reply, so she hammered harder than ever. Presently a window in the second story was cautiously opened and a head poked out and a voice called:

"Who's there?"

"Belle Boyd, and I have important intelligence to give to Colonel Ashby."

"My dear Belle!" shrieked the voice from the window. "Where in the world did you come from and how did you get here?"

"Oh, I forced the sentries," was the reply, in a matter of fact voice.

Within sixty seconds the girl was in the house and receiving refreshments and telling her strange story to her wondering friend. The horse in the meantime was taken to the stable by a negro and carefully groomed and fed. Only after these important details had been attended to was the girl permitted to tell her story.

"I must see Colonel Ashby," she said in conclusion, "and if you can tell me where to find him I will go at once."

She was informed that the Confederate officer and his party were in the woods about a half mile distant from the place in which they were sitting. Just as the girl was ready to go the front door was thrown open and Colonel Ashby stood before her. He looked at her as if she were a ghost and then finally burst forth in amazement:

"My God, Miss Belle, is that you? Where did you come from? Did you drop from the clouds?"

"No," she said smilingly, "I didn't. I came on horseback and I have some very important information."

Whereupon she related the details of the council that had taken place in the Boyd home, and then told the story of her mad ride through the night. She concluded by handing him the cipher, which he said would be communicated to his superior officers at once.

After that she insisted on mounting her horse and returning home again. It was more than two hours' ride, during which time she ran the blockade of the sleeping sentries with comparative success. Just at dawn when she was in sight of her home one of the sentries she was passing called out:

"Halt or I'll shoot!"

But she did not halt. On the contrary she whipped her horse until it fairly leaped through the air. She felt that the man was leveling his gun in her direction. She lay flat on her horse's back with her arms around his neck, and this was done in the very nick of time, for at that same moment a hot bullet came singing past her ears. That was the only serious interruption. In a few minutes she had reached the grounds surrounding the Boyd home. Fortunately no one was in sight. She hurried into the house and went to bed in her aunt's room just at the break of dawn.

Two days later, General Shields marched south with the idea of laying a trap to catch General Jackson. Once again the fearless girl determined to carry the information she possessed to her Confederate friends. Major Tyndale, at that time Provost Marshal, gave Belle Boyd and her cousin a pass to Winchester. Once there a gentleman of standing in the community called on her and handing her a package, said:

"Miss Belle, I am going to ask you to take these letters, and send them through the lines to the Confederate army. One of them is of supreme importance and I beseech you to try and get it safely to General Jackson."

After the exercise of considerable ingenuity she managed to get a pass to Front Royal. To add to the romantic feature of the business a young Union officer, who admired the girl, offered to escort her to her destination. They went in a carriage, but before starting she made it a point to conceal the Jackson letter inside her dress. The other letters, which were of comparatively small importance, she handed to the Union officer with the remark that she would take them from him when they reached Front Royal. On the way, as she feared, they were stopped by a sentinel. The Union admirer of the Confederate spy explained that they had a pass which would permit them to proceed on their way, but the zealous sentinel insisted on searching them and was highly indignant when he discovered the compromising letters in the hands of the young man. He insisted upon confiscating them, but in the excitement forgot all about the girl, and she was permitted to go unmolested, carrying with her the precious letter intended for General Jackson.

Afterwards she laughingly expressed contrition for having involved an ardent admirer in such a serious plight, but excused herself on the ground that all was fair in war as well as in love. Fortunately, the young man, who was a perfectly loyal Northern soldier, was given the credit of having discovered the papers, which were valuable to his superior officers. Thus do we sometimes make a virtue of necessity.

After Belle Boyd had been in Front Royal for several days she learned that the Confederates were coming to that place, but she also discovered that General Banks was at Strasbourg with 4,000 men; that White was at Harper's Ferry; Shields and Geary a short distance away, and Frémont below the valley. At a spot which was the vital point all of the separate divisions were expected to meet and cooperate in the destruction of General Jackson. She realized that the Confederates were in a most critical situation and that unless the officers in command were aware of the facts they might rush into a trap which meant possible annihilation.

With characteristic promptness she decided on her plan of action. She rushed out to warn the approaching Confederates. On that occasion she wore a dark blue dress with a fancy white apron over it which made her a shining mark for bullets. The Federal pickets fired at her but missed and a shell burst near her at one time, but she threw herself flat on the ground and thus escaped what seemed to be sure death. Presently she came within sight of the approaching Confederates and waved her bonnet as a signal.

Major Harry Douglass, whom she knew, galloped up and received from her the information, which he immediately transmitted to General Jackson. The result of all this was a rout of the Union forces.

It was in this battle of Bull Run which followed soon afterwards that General Bee, as he rallied his men, shouted:

"There's Jackson standing like a stone wall!"

From that time, as has been aptly said, the name he received in a baptism of fire displaced, that which he had received in a baptism of water.

The number of Union men engaged in the battle of Bull Run was about 18,000, and the number of Confederates somewhat greater.

Soon after the engagement the young woman received the following letter, which she prized until the hour of her death.

Miss Belle Boyd:
I thank you for myself and for the army, for the immense service you have rendered your country today.
Hastily, I am your friend,
T. J. Jackson, C. S. A.

Shortly before the close of the war, Belle Boyd was captured and imprisoned. She escaped and made her way to England. In London, she attracted the attention of George Augustus Sala, the famous writer. She had been married in the meantime and her husband, Lieutenant Hardage of the Confederate army, was among those taken prisoner by the Union forces.

While abroad she became financially embarrassed; indeed, at one time she was reduced to actual want. A stranger in a strange land, sick in mind and body, she was in a pitiable condition. Mr. Sala wrote a letter to the London Times explaining her sad state and roundly abusing the United States Government which had, he said, not only imprisoned her husband but was also "barbarous enough to place him in irons."

British sympathies were very strongly with the South at that time, and as a result of this plea provision was made for the immediate wants of the famous spy. After the war she disappeared from the public gaze, and some years later died in comparative obscurity.

2

The Indian scout who was the hero of King Philip War

It is a curious fact that Job Kattenanit, one of the Praying Indians of Deer Island, in Boston Harbor, should have emerged from King Philip's war with more glory than any other man, either white or red, who participated in that bloody contest.

Like the historic Biblical character from whom he received his name, Job was a sorely afflicted man. He was among the first group of Indians in that section of the United States to accept the Christian religion, and it was this fact, and in order to distinguish them from the other red men, that Kattenanit and his companions received the designation of the Praying Indians.

It is regrettable to record, however, that the excesses of some of the other natives had caused an indiscriminate hatred of the Indians throughout New England. They were regarded as wild beasts who should be shot and killed without mercy. It was while this feeling was at its height that Job Kattenanit and eleven of his companions were arrested on a charge of being concerned in the murder of seven white men. They were captured in the town of Lancaster and brought to Boston, tied "neck and neck," as the practice was in36 those primitive days. The evidence against them was of the flimsiest character, and it was only through the efforts of Captain John Gookin, a magistrate who felt a special interest in the Indians, that their lives were spared and they were condemned to imprisonment on Deer Island.

In the meantime King Philip, the Indian chieftain, was spreading terror among the white people. He was jealous of their gradual encroachment upon what he conceived to be his domain and he planned to destroy them. He was a man of sagacity, although said to be wanting in physical courage, and he gradually combined all of the Indian tribes into one strong confederation and waited for a chance to strike the decisive blow.

It came at Swansea on Sunday, July 4, 1675. The settlers were going to church when the Indians suddenly burst upon them. But these pioneers were both pious and prepared, and taking up arms they routed their assailants. Philip and his warriors then hunted the settlers in the Connecticut valley, burning down their homes and subjecting the people to the most atrocious forms of cruelty. In the spring the war broke out anew along a frontier of three hundred miles and to within twenty miles of Boston. The Indians had remained quiet for a long time after the initial outbreak – so quiet that the whites were thoroughly alarmed. They knew the ruthless nature of their foes and they feared the consequences to the women and children if they should be taken unawares.

It was at this critical stage of affairs that Major Gookin – he had been promoted – bethought himself of the Praying Indians on Deer Island. It was absolutely necessary to know something of the plans of King Philip and his bloodthirsty redskins. If a white man went into their camp he was certain to be scalped and tortured. If an Indian could be induced to act as a spy he might save the whites from a wholesale massacre.

The eloquent Major visited Deer Island and presented these facts to the prisoners and called for volunteers. He said that a service of this kind would not only secure the release of the Praying Indians, but would win for them the lasting friendship of the white people.

"I go," said one handsome brave, rising and lifting his hand solemnly in mid-air. "I go, not for reward, but to save the palefaces from death."

The Indian was Job Kattenanit. He was tall and perfectly erect, with piercing black eyes and a grave, almost sorrowful countenance. There was a suggestion of nobility in his bearing. In short, he might well have passed for the original of Deerfoot, so vividly pictured by James Fenimore Cooper.

Major Gookin recognized him at once. He knew the Indians personally, and he had a special friendship for this straight shouldered chap. He rushed over and gripped him by the hand.

"Job," he exclaimed, "the white people shall know of this and in time it will help your people."

A mist passed before the bright eyes of the Indian, and he gave a gesture as if to sweep the suggestion aside.

"White man cruel to Indian," he rejoined, "but the red man must return good for evil."

As they were about to leave another Indian rose in his place and said:

"Me go, too – me go with Job."

This was James Quannapohit, a native in whom Major Gookin also had implicit confidence. After deliberation he decided to accept the services of both volunteers. They were taken aside and given careful directions.

That night Job and James were brought secretly from Deer Island and set free – according to arrangement. In order to avoid difficulties they had been first escorted beyond the British lines.

From that point they journeyed alone and on foot. It was a long walk, and when they reached their destination they were footsore, hungry and almost in rags. It was as they wished. They bore the appearance of fugitives, of escaped prisoners. It was daybreak when they arrived in the camp of the Nipmuck Indians. They threw themselves on their faces and begged for food and drink. The amazed redskins who surrounded them wanted to know who they were and what they were doing in the camp of the Nipmuck Indians. Job, who acted as spokesman, insisted upon refreshments and said he would tell his story to someone in authority. After their wants had been satisfied they were escorted to Mantampe, a chief Sachem of the tribe.

"What you do here?" he demanded.

"We have escaped from the clutches of the white man," replied Job in his native tongue, "and we came to you for protection. The white man of Lancaster came and took the red man prisoner. He charged us with murdering his squaws and he gave us no chance to defend ourselves."

"Tell me more," said the chief Sachem, deeply interested.

Job did as he was requested and he was able to do so all the more eloquently because he was giving an account of some things that had actually occurred to the Praying Indians. He said they had been accused by David, a fellow savage, of being concerned in the murder of the whites. But he added that the manner in which David was forced to make this charge robbed it of all value. He related how Colonel Mosely and a scouting party captured David and tied him to a tree; how with six muskets pointed at his head he was told to confess or die. To save his life he named eleven men he understood were present at the murder, though he himself was not there, and knew nothing about it. The men were put on trial, and so great and indiscriminate was the popular feeling against the natives that several of them were condemned.

"But you are alive," grinned the Sachem.

Job admitted the soft impeachment and explained how he and his companions had been imprisoned on Deer Island. He said that he and James Quannapohit had managed to escape, but slyly enough neglected to tell the Sachem that the escape had been arranged by their English friends. He concluded by saying that they had come to the camp of the Nipmuck Indians to get the lay of the land, "so that they might advise the friends they had left if it would be possible for them also to escape."

The Sachem accepted the story of Job and his companion and they were given the liberty of the camp. The two Praying Indians kept their eyes and ears open and learned much. Mantampe was undoubtedly in command of a large force. Job met many of the Indians, who were, as a rule, able fighting men, straight as arrows, very tall and active.

Three squaws who were in the camp interested and amused the spies. One was a very proud dame. She spent the best part of each day in dressing herself in all the colors of the rainbow; she powdered her hair and painted her face, wore numberless necklaces, had jewels in her hair and bracelets on her wrists. When she finished her toilet she sat down and spent the remainder of the day in making girdles of wampum and beads.

James Quannapohit found great favor in the eyes of Mantampe. He made him share his tent with him and insisted upon his repeating the story of his escape from Deer Island. During the course of these talks James learned that the Nipmuck Indians contemplated a raid on the white settlers. They proposed to burn Lancaster and then attack other towns. The method of the raid was not made clear. One morning Mantampe called James before him.

"Son," he said in substance, "I am about to take a journey for the purpose of visiting the big chief, King Philip. If all goes well I may take you with me."

This alarmed James. He dreaded the idea of going further into the Indian country, perhaps to a point where it would be impossible for him to make his escape. Besides that he had a good reason for wishing to avoid a meeting with the king. He had once fought against Philip at Mount Hope. He had taken a conspicuous part in the battle and he knew that if the King recognized him he would be shot.

The next morning he arose before any one was stirring, and left the camp. He urged Job to go along with him but the other spy refused to do so.

"But you will be killed," urged James, "when they discover my absence. They will at once suspect that you are a spy, and that means death."

Job shook his head.

"You go," he said. "I don't blame you for that. But I am going to stay for a while. It may mean life or death, but I am willing to take my chances."

Nothing that James could say would shake the determination of Job. So the younger Indian started on the return journey to Boston alone. There had been severe storms and the snow lay deep on the ground. It was necessary for the Indian to wear heavy snowshoes and this made traveling all the more difficult.

When the Indian spy reached Boston he had a tale of unparalleled hardships to relate to his white friends. But more important than that was his story of the plans of the Indians against the settlers in and around Lancaster. He was highly praised for the effective work he had done and was showered with attentions by the white men and their families. For the first time since the beginning of what is popularly known as King Philip's war an Indian was treated as though he were a human being.

Indeed, it is no exaggeration to state that the exploit of the two Indians did more to reinstate the redskins in the good graces of the whites than anything that had occurred in years.

But curiously enough the settlers did little or nothing to protect themselves against the expected attack. The very warning which should have put them on their guard seemed to lull them into a false sense of security. There were two reasons for this. The first one was that the suspected danger was comparatively remote – a matter of weeks in fact. Another and more important one was the desire to get further and fuller information from the other Indian scout. Job was the shrewder and more capable of the two messengers. It was just possible that the abrupt departure of James might arouse the suspicion of the savages and cause them to entirely revise their plans. James was closely questioned concerning his companion.

"Why didn't he come back with you?" he was asked.

James shrugged his shoulders and threw out his hands in a gesture of hopelessness.

"He very stubborn man. Have his own way. No listen to poor James."

"Do you think he intends to come back?"

At this suggestion of possible disloyalty on the part of his friend the Indian became very indignant. He was so angry that he found it impossible to express himself coherently. But his manner, if not his words, perfectly satisfied the questioner of the perfect good faith of Job. As a matter of fact it was never seriously doubted and the white man who propounded the query felt ashamed at having put the unworthy suspicion into words.

In the meantime Job found himself in an embarrassing and really dangerous situation. With the flight of James the savages, for the first time, became skeptical concerning the motives of the two visitors. The chief Sachem sent for Job and put him through a severe cross-examination. But Job was shrewd and told them a cock-and-bull story that satisfied their curiosity. As a result of this he was treated with even more consideration than when he first arrived in camp. He was fearful lest the Sachem should want him to accompany him on the proposed visit to King Philip. He knew that to go before the big Chief would be taking his life in his hands. Finally, to his great joy, the Sachem decided that he should not go on the trip.

The next three days were days of great anxiety to the spy. He knew that the emissary to the King would bring final plans for the attack on the whites and he was fearful lest anything should happen to deprive him of this much needed information. So he exerted himself to the utmost in order to keep the good will of the savages. As a result of this they virtually took him to their bosoms. In speaking of this afterwards he said that he felt no compunctions of conscience. He did not feel that he was betraying them but rather that he was engaged in an honest attempt to save human life.

He took part in their amusements, which helped to while away the time. One of the most popular of the games was called "hunt the button," a diversion somewhat akin to that which is enjoyed by children the world over. This was played at night when the natives, in paint and buckskin, seated themselves around a tepee, with the fire blazing bright in their faces, as they swung their hands in time with a rhythmic chant. This was indulged in by both sexes. Also they played the game of "deer-foot." In this a number of cylindrical bones, usually taken from the foot of the deer, and perforated with several holes around their sides, were strung on a cord, which had at one end several strands of beads and at the other a long needle. The object was to toss the string, with the beads upon it, in such a way as to catch in the point of the needle, which was retained in the hand, any designated one of the bones or bead strands.

KING PHILIP, OR METACOMET.

But presently the Sachem returned from his visit to the King and from the air of activity which prevailed, Job realized that something important was on hand. It did not take him long to find out that that something was war. Clubs that were armed with jagged teeth of stone were brought from their hiding places and sharpened. Javelins, lances and arrows became very much in evidence. The arrows were most numerous. They were made of hard wood and with a feather from the eagle. These various weapons were not unknown to Job, of course, but his own tribe was composed of more peace-loving Indians and they were not in the habit of using the more destructive weapons.

Finally one night the Sachem gathered the most important men of the tribe about him and outlined the plans of King Philip. Job, who was still in the confidence of the savages, was permitted to hear all that was said. The proposal was shocking, even to a redskin. The intention was to destroy the whites at one blow, if that were possible. The day and the hour at which the descent was to be made upon Lancaster was fixed and the method of attack outlined. This was news indeed, and vastly more important than that which had been carried to Boston by James.

Job Kattenanit knew that the hour had come to act. With haste he would have time to warn the threatened settlers, but with not a minute to spare. Creeping away, he made for the edge of the camp. Fortunately most of the Indians – aside from those who were attending the council of war – were asleep. He passed one sentinel unobserved and gained the fringe of the encampment in safety. The road to Boston was familiar to him and he counted on reaching there by dusk on the evening of February 8th.

But just as he struck the main road leading to his destination there was a cry of anger and dismay from the Nipmuck camp.

His flight had been discovered.

Instead of halting he redoubled his speed. From time to time he heard savage cries and he knew that he was being pursued. The thought of giving up never once entered his mind. It was too late to retreat now. The Nipmuck Indians had been credulous enough, but it would be impossible to deceive them any longer. Job was in fine physical condition and he ran with the swiftness of a deer. But his enemies were equally fleet-footed and it seemed only a question of time when he would be overtaken. Nearer and nearer came the footsteps in the rear. He felt that there must be a number of Indians in the party, but evidently they did not have time to give a general alarm.

Just when he was congratulating himself on the possibility of outrunning his pursuers an arrow whizzed past his head. This was a new danger and one that he had not anticipated. He paused for a second and turned to look at the men who were after him. Instantly a well-directed arrow struck him in the chest within an inch of the region of the heart.

A heavy blanket covered the fleeing redskin, and with that momentary pause and turn the arrow had penetrated the covering. But, as by a miracle, it went no further. The Praying Indian wore a metal charm on his breast, suspended by a string fastened about his neck. That saved his life.

In that trying moment the shrewd Indian made his resolution. To pull the arrow out and run ahead again only meant postponing the inevitable. Instead of that, he paused motionless for a second, then swayed to and fro, and fell flat on his back.

Everything depended upon the success of this ruse. It was, perhaps, half a minute before the Nipmuck Indians came up, and when they did they regarded the motionless body with something like awe. Job suppressed his breathing as much as possible. Two of the pursuers engaged in an animated conversation, and finally turning, retraced their steps, leaving the spy for dead.

He lay there perfectly quiet until he was sure they were out of sight. Then he jumped up and resumed his interrupted flight. The story of that journey through a wilderness in the most inclement season of the year should rank with the classics of adventure. But only the savage himself knew what he was compelled to undergo, and he never spoke of it afterwards.

He arrived at Major Gookin's house late on the night of February 9th. His feet were bruised and bleeding from the long trip and he was faint from weakness on account of exposure and want of food. All of the inmates at the Gookin dwelling were asleep and Job had to rap repeatedly on the door to awaken them. Presently the Major came downstairs and the meeting between the two – white man and the red – was most affecting.

The tidings he brought were startling. It was evident that it would only be a question of hours before the settlers were attacked. Major Gookin did not return to his bed that night. He dispatched messengers to all of the surrounding towns. In an incredibly short time troops were marching from everywhere to the aid of the threatened town. Captain Wadsworth, at Marlborough, received the news at daybreak and started for Lancaster at once. Others did the same thing.

The savages came over four hundred strong. Re-enforcements added to this number. The white men were not so numerous, but they fought with a courage born of desperation. The town was partially destroyed by fire and a few of the people taken prisoners by the Indians. Had it not been for the warning of Job Kattenanit there would have been a wholesale massacre and Lancaster would have been left in ashes.

That was the beginning of the end. Driven to drastic measures by the atrocities of the savages, the settlers hunted down the Indians like wild beasts. King Philip was driven from one hiding place to another, going finally to his old home on Mount Hope, Rhode Island, where he was shot by a faithless Indian, August 12, 1676.

But Job Kattenanit, the Praying Indian, did more than any white man to break up the reign of terror caused by the savages, and even though history fails to mention the fact, he was the real hero of King Philip's War.

3

Doctor Steiber and the mystery of the Franco-Prussian war

One of the mysteries that has ever puzzled patriotic Frenchmen is how Germany – in 1870 – was able to crush France in one of the shortest and most humiliating wars in history. The bravery, the unquestioned courage of the French soldier, in every war prior to and since 1870, has been universally conceded. The French troops have often held out against great odds and acknowledged defeat only after a long and stubborn resistance. Why did the national defenses in 1870 fall down like so many houses of cards? Why was France caught in such an utterly unprepared condition? Why was it that so many French troops were captured like rats in a trap? In a word, what was the mystery of the Franco-Prussian War?

The answer is simple. They were out-spied, and the man behind the mystery was Doctor Steiber, Chief of the Prussian Secret Service.

He confessed afterwards, and it has since been corroborated from many reliable sources, that two armies were responsible for the defeat of France in the Franco-Prussian War. One was Steiber's army of spies which invaded the country in 1867, 1868, and 1869, and the other was the German military army which came in 1870.

Steiber was a man with untiring push, unlimited persistence and an unpleasant personality. He had big ears, a big nose, shifty eyes and an irritating smile. Like a certain character made famous by Dickens, he was always washing his hands in invisible water. He was cordially disliked by many of the German officers, but was a favorite of Prince Bismarck, and that, of course, turned the scales in his favor. Napoleon's chief spy was an Alsatian smuggler, while Bismarck's secret service agent was a socialist. At least that is what he was before he attracted the attention of the German Prime Minister. After that he believed absolutely in the sacred rights of property.

It was in 1864 that he first performed any work of consequence outside of Germany. About that time Bismarck began to have designs upon Bohemia, but before attacking that country the prudent head of the State Department desired to get all of the inside information that was possible. He looked about him for an instrument, and his gaze fell upon the erstwhile socialist.

In the latter part of 1864 Steiber set out for Bohemia. As the people of that country were very religious he went in the guise of a peddler of religious statues. He traveled from one town to another gaining the confidence of the honest and simple minded people, and acquiring a vast fund of information concerning the forts and defenses and the general state of military preparedness – or unpreparedness. He remained there for many months and had the assistance of a number of lesser spies. When he returned to Germany he was able to place this data in the hands of Bismarck, who, in turn, gave it to Moltke.

On the strength of this report it was decided to invade Bohemia, and many thousands of well-drilled, well-officered and well-fed troops advanced upon what might fairly be called a helpless country. It was one victory after another until Bohemia was entirely subjugated. Doctor Steiber accompanied the German army in its victorious march, but more in the role of an informer than a warrior. Naturally many of the German officers were aware of the character of his work, and some of them were outspoken in their disgust. Many of them refused to eat at the same mess with him. Bismarck was in the field on one occasion and Steiber complained to him of the affronts that had been placed upon him.

"They go out of their way to show their dislike of me," he said.

"Well, what of it?" was the gruff query.

"They should be disciplined," he insisted, "because I am merely carrying out your orders."

"You think so?"

"I do."

"Well," was the shrewd response, "I will teach them a lesson in my own way."

And so he did. And it took the form of having Doctor Steiber dine with him in his own tent.

During the course of the invasion Steiber was made Governor of Braum, the capital of Moravia, thus becoming a sort of glorified chief of police. In this position, as might be expected, there were many rich pickings, a fact that was not overlooked by the thrifty ex-socialist. This was not all. He was decorated, and the medal bestowed upon him was pinned on his ample bosom by Moltke. That soldier, like Bismarck, was eminently practical. As if to justify himself he said on one occasion:

"One must not confine oneself to giving money to spies. One must know how to show them honor when they deserve it."

After the Bohemian business had been concluded, Doctor Steiber had a period of comparative ease. He rested, so to speak, on his "laurels." He prospered in a worldly sense, and was happy in possessing the confidence and the favor of those who were high in Prussian officialdom. He knew the time would come when his peculiar services would be in demand. Meanwhile he continued with the routine work of the Secret Service office. The call for bigger things came sooner than he anticipated. It was early one day in June, 1867, that he received a summons from Bismarck.

He dropped everything and hastened to the home of the Prime Minister. He found him alone, and at breakfast. Bismarck greeted him with lazy, good natured tolerance, and bade him be seated until he had finished, what was to him at that moment the most important thing in the world – his meal. While Steiber waited he had a chance to study the personality of this remarkable man.

It seemed to him that Bismarck was all body. He was impressed more than anything else with the bulkiness of the

Prime Minister. He was massive, – "as big as a mountain," as he afterwards expressed it. For the rest of it, there was nothing to dispel the popular conception of the man, the broad shoulders, thick neck, grisly mustache, bushy eyebrows and grim determined look.

"Steiber," said the Prime Minister between bites, "we have real work cut out for you now – work and not mere child's play."

"And might I inquire what it is, your Excellency?" asked the spy respectfully.

"All in good time," was the playful response. "For the present you will see that we have important business on hand."

This allusion to the meal spread before the man of blood and iron, of course, brought the expected laugh from the Chief of the Prussian Secret Service. And he sat and watched with amazement the gastronomic powers of the great man. He had heard of Bismarck's ability in this line, but had never witnessed anything like the present exhibition. He had been told that on one historic occasion, in the presence of the Emperor, the count drained a quart of champagne from a loving cup without pausing for breath, and now he believed it.

The breakfast which was to satisfy the morning appetite of Bismarck was an average meal – the kind that ordinarily pleased him. It consisted of six eggs, a beefsteak, several slices of pheasant, a dish of fried potatoes, a plate of rye bread, cakes, three cups of coffee and a quart of red wine. Two large hunting dogs hovered about the table, and from time to time during the meal the Prime Minister tossed bits of meat to them. After he had concluded his breakfast Bismarck leaned back in his chair with a sigh of satisfaction. Presently he reached for a long-stemmed pipe, and lighting it, sent clouds of smoke about the room. He was at peace with all the world – and with Bismarck, too.

"Now," he said lazily, and yet with a sort of determination, "for business."

Steiber realized, when his patron arose, that Bismarck was a tall man, a fact that was not always apparent because of his great bulk. The Prime Minister laid his pipe aside and paced the floor as he talked. Presently he sat down again and lit a cigar. And during the remainder of the interview he continued smoking. He was what is popularly called a "chain smoker," each cigar being lighted by the stub of its predecessor.

His instructions were clean cut and to the point. Steiber was to go into France and spy out that country for the benefit of Prussia. He was to have unlimited means and all of the assistance he might require. He was to get plans of forts and defenses generally; to ascertain the size and condition of the French army and to learn all that was possible of the secrets of the French War Office. In a word, he was to repeat, in France, what he had already done in Bohemia.

PRINCE VON BISMARCK

When Bismarck dismissed Steiber the spy had the greatest commission of his career. He had little doubt of his ability to execute it. He feared no man, except possibly Bismarck. The meeting and the parting of the two men on that eventful day might be called historic. The Chancellor even went so far as to lay his hand on the shoulder of his agent.

"Remember the Fatherland!"

The builder of the German Empire stood there with all of the immensity and impressiveness of a bronze statue, and as the spy left he carried with him the remembrance of the tall figure, the broad shoulders, the thick neck, the grisly mustache, the keen eyes, and the grim, determined look. And as a background there was the table littered with the remains of that amazing meal and the Japanned plate filled with smoldering cigar stumps.

Steiber went forth proud and boastful and with the vision of more medals to cover his ample breast. His big ears seemed to become bigger, his enormous nose appeared to grow larger, and his shifty eyes were fairly dancing with delight.

He hurried to his office and began to prepare for the campaign of espionage. It was not the sort of thing to plan in an hour or a day. He devoted weeks of labor to the task. Maps of all kinds were consulted and all sorts of secret information was brought from all sorts of impossible hiding-places. He considered next the men that should go with him and the various branches of work that should be assigned to them, and finally the job was completed with the thoroughness for which the official German is noted.

When Steiber started on this secret invasion of France he took with him two lieutenants, Zernicki and Kalten. Their work lay in the military line. They visited fortifications in all parts of France; they carried cameras with them, and in spite of the regulations forbidding such things, they made photographs of the defenses and even of the cannon in the forts. Disguised as peddlers they made their way into the various garrisons and studied the methods of the drill, discovered the number of men attached to each of the regiments, and altogether obtained a mass of information that could not possibly have been gleaned from blue books or official publications.

In the same manner men were sent to the different navy yards. They explored the warships and cruisers and obtained data which was promptly forwarded to the Foreign Office in Berlin. Napoleon III reigned over France at this time, and while he must have known the danger that threatened his country by reason of German aggression, he apparently made no effort to avert it. Spies ran about almost under his nose and he could not see them. Some years before this, when it was reported that the people of Paris were discontented, he said:

"Well, gild the dome of Les Invalides – that will give them something to look at."

And, indeed, he gave the people a great deal to distract them from the fear of both poverty and war. He was largely responsible for making Paris the most beautiful city in the world. He laid out the magnificent boulevards, built the great sewers and in other ways made the city the joy and pride of the inhabitants.

There had long been ill feeling smoldering between France and Germany and the two countries were on the verge of war in 1866. But this significant fact was lost on Napoleon III, and the German spies, when they came into France, found a fertile soil to cultivate.

Steiber did not stop at learning the secrets of the army and navy. His spies even went to Versailles and were to be found in public and semi-public institutions everywhere. They consisted of both men and women. If one went into a restaurant the waiter who attended to his wants was likely to be a German spy. If a Frenchwoman – possibly the wife of an army or naval officer – went to her dressmaker's she was fitted by a female who probably was on the payroll of Doctor Steiber. At one time, it is hinted, there were five thousand Prussian spies working on French territory. Never was a country so overrun by the secret agents of a foreign power.

Finally, in the latter part of 1869, Steiber completed his work and started back to Berlin. And all this time the complacent French Emperor and the credulous French people, were in ignorance of how they had been betrayed by the thousands of foreign visitors. Steiber, Zernicki and Kalten carried several large trunks with them – trunks that were zealously guarded by day and by night. These trunks contained plans of all sorts and reports that had been returned by the myriads of spies under the Chief of the Prussian Secret Service. Suppose these trunks had been captured and confiscated by the French police? Suppose Steiber and his emissaries had been arrested while they were still on French territory? Is it too much to say that it would have changed the course of history?

Steiber on his return to Berlin went direct to the home of the Chancellor. He found him, as before, resting after one of those meals for which he was famous. It seemed very familiar, the broad shoulders, thick neck, grisly mustache, bushy eyebrows and grim, determined look. He greeted his agent with a playful manner and bade him tell all he knew. That consumed some time, for it must be remembered that Steiber and his corps of assistants had spent more than two years in France. It is true that much of the information had been sent as fast as it was collected, but Bismarck wanted direct, first-hand news from his trusted servant.

And while he talked the Chancellor smoked one cigar after another and occasionally tossed bits of meat to the dogs that were constantly by his side. After the interview Steiber received another medal to add to the collection he had already acquired. And then Berlin, so to speak, having set the stage, calmly awaited the course of events.

The climax came quicker than was anticipated. Napoleon demanded that the King of Prussia should bind himself by an autograph letter never to support Prince Leopold as a candidate for the Spanish crown. Bismarck, confident in his power, and fortified by the knowledge that he had of the French unpreparedness, calmly refused to lay the request before the monarch.

This was an intolerable slight from one who was regarded as a subordinate. A few days after this the French Ambassador chanced to meet the King in a public walk at Ems, and there and then asked him to give the desired promise. King William refused, with indignation, to transact business under such circumstances and later notified the Ambassador that he would not be given an audience at the royal palace.

Napoleon regarded this as the insult direct, and as a consequence of the incident war was declared between the two countries. The people, of course, were unfamiliar with real conditions. They did not know that their country had been infested with foreign spies and that they were utterly unprepared for war. They were angered at the apparent slight that had been put upon the French nation and they were filled with a burning patriotism. In no time the streets of Paris were filled with but one cry:

"On to Berlin!"

Napoleon, heading a hastily mobilized army, marched north and camped at Metz, whence he proposed crossing the Rhine into Germany. But the Germans, instead of waiting for this, invaded France, hurrying directly toward Paris. The scorn and indignation of the people was intense. Marshal McMahon fought bravely, but was driven back, and Marshal Bazaine, after a struggle, was driven within the fortifications at Metz. Everything had come about as the Germans anticipated. A large part of the French army was shut up in a trap, while the remainder struggled for existence.

On the eve of the first of September, 1870, the King of Prussia arrived at Versailles and took up his lodgings in the palace belonging to the Duc de Persigny. And with him was Doctor Steiber, gloating and continually washing his hands in invisible water. Was not all of this his work? Had he not spied out the land? Had he not invaded France before the army arrived? In a word, was not this conquest of the army but a confirmation of his victory of espionage? He was more boastful than ever and his big ears and big nose were everywhere in evidence.

While the King of Prussia ruled like a conqueror, Steiber played the tyrant in his own way. He had large powers and he did not hesitate to use them. One incident will show the character of the man. A wealthy and popular young Frenchman, Monsieur de Raynal, had returned to Versailles from his honeymoon, arriving just in time to meet the German invaders. He kept a diary of the happenings of the invasion. It was not much – merely a colorful account, day by day, of the doings of the invaders. Perhaps he did not draw a flattering picture of the Prussians. How could he? The confiscation of the offending document and maybe the temporary imprisonment of the writer would have been ample punishment, if indeed, any were necessary. But the beggar on horseback did not think so.

He decreed that the gallant Frenchman should be executed. Friends of the gentleman interceded and asked clemency on the ground that he was but newly married and on his honeymoon. Steiber spread out his big hands, shrugged his ugly shoulders and said, "Ah, but that only makes my task the more painful." Even the German soldiers entered their protest. But in spite of it Monsieur de Raynal was executed. And Steiber rubbed his hands, washing them, as ever, in invisible water. But all the water in creation would not wash the blood of innocent victims from those dirty hands!

While this was going on in Versailles the brave McMahon was pressing forward to the relief of Bazaine. Presently he reached Sedan, where a great battle was fought, resulting in the decisive defeat of the French. On the evening of the following day Napoleon – Napoleon the Little – as he was derisively called by Victor Hugo – sent a letter to the King of Prussia in which he said:

"Not being able to die at the head of my troops, I can only resign my sword into the hands of Your Majesty."

Following this, Napoleon, with McMahon and 80,000 prisoners of war, surrendered to the enemy. Three days later the Emperor was deposed and France made a Republic. So rapidly did one event follow another. Bazaine held out until October when he, with 6,000 officers and 170,000 men, laid down their arms. Bazaine was afterwards tried and sentenced to degradation and death for having failed in his duty to France. The sentence was commuted to twenty years' imprisonment, from which he effected his escape.

Then came the Third Republic, the siege of Paris and the treaty of peace in February, 1871; France agreed to give up all of German-speaking Lorraine and the whole of Alsace and to pay 5,000,000,000 francs to Germany. The story of how the inhabitants of Alsace were compelled to choose between becoming German citizens or leaving the province is a sad one. The melancholy procession, when fifty thousand of them left their homes and their all and marched into France on the 30th of September, 1872, will never be forgotten.

The great statue in the Place de la Concorde in Paris, with one of its marble figures draped in mourning on national holidays, has been a constant reminder to posterity.

When the victorious Germans returned to Berlin Doctor Steiber was with them – proud and boastful as ever. The order of the Red Eagle was added to his numerous decorations, and it was reputed that he became a millionaire in addition.

The Franco-Prussian War – or at least the result of that war – has ever been a mystery to patriotic Frenchmen. But the solution of it may be found in that secret invasion of spies led by Steiber and his unscrupulous lieutenants.

4

How Monsieur de Meinau helped to make Jerome Bonaparte the King of Westphalia

Among all of the world's famous impostors it is doubtful if any could hold a candle to Monsieur de Meinau. Monsieur did not always have such a dignified name. Originally, it will be recalled, he was an Alsatian smuggler and had the plain every-day appellation of Schulmeister. But as Napoleon's chief spy his rise to fame and fortune was both sure and sudden. He was lavishly rewarded by the Man of Destiny. Indeed, his appointment as Chief of Police of Vienna was a fortune in itself and a fair return for the services he had rendered, and the dangers he had braved as the secret agent of Napoleon.

But Napoleon was not yet satisfied. He wished to be the King of Kings and to reconstruct Germany, Italy and the Netherlands. His ambition was to rule over an empire that should be encircled and guarded by a belt of dependent thrones. In pursuance of this policy he seized Naples and made his brother Joseph its king. After that he converted the Republic of the Netherlands into a monarchy, and placed his brother Louis at its head with the title of the King of Holland.

In the meantime he needed more information concerning the power and the plans of those who were opposed to his designs. At this stage of events he once more sent for his trusted spy, Schulmeister. He had made him Monsieur de Meinau, with both the title and the estates that went with it. But the new Monsieur knew his imperial patron well enough to understand that he could not rest on his laurels. With Napoleon incessant activity was the price of favor.

As the result of the interview with the Emperor Monsieur left Vienna with letters of introduction to the Austrian officers at Oedenburg. This was in west Hungary, about thirty-seven miles from the Austrian capitol. Here he learned that the Archduke Charles and Ferdinand had combined forces the day before and were preparing for a united attack on the French troops. This information was exceedingly important and he never rested until he had forwarded it to Napoleon.

After that he felt entitled to a little relaxation and he joined the Austrian officers in the gayeties of camp life. He had been hospitably received on his arrival and now was royally entertained by his new found friends. His scarred forehead and his severe military manner impressed them. Add to this the fact that he was supposed to have undergone great privations and dangers as an officer of the Austrian Secret Service and it will not be difficult to understand why the soldiers insisted upon placing a halo of romance around his head. A dinner was given in his honor and on this occasion the rascal actually entertained his hosts with stories of some of his thrilling adventures in the service of the Fatherland. His methods were simple enough. He related real exploits, merely picturing himself as an Austrian secret agent instead of a spy of Napoleon. His narratives were received with applause and manifestations of delight.

The Austrians had been at Oedenburg for some time and the pleasures of camp life were beginning to affect the discipline of the men. Schulmeister, or rather Monsieur de Meinau, was ordinarily a person of abstemious habits, but he could be a jolly good fellow when the occasion demanded it, and this, you may be sure, was one of the occasions. The flowing bowl was passed around so often that it was in grave danger of flowing over. The more wine the officers drank the greater became their affection for the spy. They literally threw themselves around his neck, which was quite a generous thing to do when we consider that under the military customs of the time they would have been justified in placing a rope around that same neck. But there was one man at the banqueting board who was a death's head at the feast. Lieutenant Bernstein looked and felt unhappy. He did not share the confidence of his comrades in Monsieur de Meinau. In fact, he frankly regarded him as a fraud. So he sat there eating little and drinking less and wondering how he could bring the spy to grief.

His opportunity came sooner than he expected. Monsieur de Meinau, having reduced his hosts to a state of semi-intoxication, hastened out to send further information to Napoleon. With his usual cleverness he had established a chain of communication between Oedenburg and Vienna. He had his own sub-spies within and without the lines of the enemy, and thus had a method of forwarding his dispatches which would have been envied by modern news associations in times of war. But on this one occasion he reckoned without his host – or at least this particular host. Bernstein was at his very heels, and when he saw him pass the slips of paper into the hands of a confederate, felt that it was time for some one to interfere. Consequently when Monsieur de Meinau returned to the banqueting board Bernstein pointed an accusing finger in his direction and exclaimed:

"I denounce that man as a spy!"

There was a loud shout of laughter at this and the man nearest to him punched the accuser in the ribs.

"Why, old man, there's nothing startling in that. We know that he is a spy."

Monsieur de Meinau folded his arms and looked the lieutenant in the eye.

"The comrade is trying to have a jest at my expense. Gentlemen, you all know that I am a spy. I have told you myself. Perhaps it was an indiscretion, but—"

"No! No!" cried Bernstein, excitedly. "Not that kind of a spy. I say that he is a spy against Austria. He has been in communication with the French troops. I caught him in the act of sending messages through the lines."

Silence fell upon the group of officers surrounding the two men. The force of the accusation was startling – so startling that it sobered them at once. A bucket of water thrown into each of their faces would not have been half so shocking. All of them turned to Monsieur de Meinau. His face was pale, but he did not lose his composure. He was ready for whatever might happen. The chief officer cried sternly:

"What have you to say to this?"

Monsieur de Meinau's arms were still folded in the way in which he had often seen Napoleon fold his arms.

"Gentlemen," he said with dignity, "I have been grossly insulted, and under the circumstances I can only do one thing – I demand an instant investigation of the accusation against me. I insist upon a trial – a court martial, if you will."

The audacity of this request had the expected result. It disarmed suspicion at the outset. And his insistence upon a trial only served to strengthen him in the minds of the officers. He was given a trial, but it was largely a perfunctory affair. The lieutenant who made the accusation was, of course, unable to prove his charge. The only witnesses against Schulmeister had fled, and he was triumphantly acquitted. He displayed numerous letters, some real and others forged, to prove that he was a patriot working in the Austrian Secret Service. General Wilhing, who presided over the trial, was profuse in his apologies and insisted upon giving him a letter to the Archduke Charles who was then at Koermoend.

Monsieur de Meinau proceeded gayly on his way to 180 the headquarters of the Archduke, arriving with his letters and his never-failing audacity. His Austrian uniform, of course, was an immense asset, which he did not fail to utilize to the fullest extent. He was not only in the confidence of the Austrians, but also in the position of being a "vindicated" man. Thereafter no one could have the temerity to point the finger of suspicion in his direction. Any charge they might make would have the appearance of being a stale and exploded slander. The most important thing for him now was not to be caught in the commission of any overt act.

Most military spies come to grief by having dispatches and documents on their person. Monsieur de Meinau knew this, and he made it his business to get rid of incriminating documents at the earliest possible moment. But yet there were times when papers and documents were his chief stock in trade. He was cordially received at Koermoend and was taken to the Archduke Charles by a member of that General's staff. The nobleman greeted the newcomer kindly and asked him for information regarding the enemy. Monsieur de Meinau having just come from Vienna via Oedenburg was able to give the Archduke some very interesting news. The fact that the greater part of it was the product of his vivid imagination did not make it any the less thrilling. As a consequence of this the Archduke regarded him with unusual favor.

This fact was not lost on the lesser lights of the camp at Koermoend. The chief-of-staff of the Archduke conceived that one who was so highly regarded by his superior was entitled to special attention at his hand. So he invited him to be his guest during his brief stay at the headquarters of the Archduke. Schulmeister – to give him his old name for the moment – accepted cheerfully, but reminded his host that he was a very busy man and that he might be compelled at any moment to leave him abruptly and without notice. This was the solemn truth, but, of course, the humor of it was lost on the chief-of-staff.

Now the General had his headquarters in a roomy frame building not far from that of the Archduke. His office was in a large apartment on the first floor. Here he kept all of his papers and military correspondence. Monsieur de Meinau – to get back to his formal designation – made note of all this and was quick to see where the soldier placed the keys of the place. For some days now he followed a policy of watchful waiting. He was a persistent man, but also a patient one. He felt sure that his opportunity would come – and it did.

One morning the Archduke decided to make an inspection of his troops. This was an all-day job and he was naturally accompanied by his chief-of-staff. When they were out of sight and hearing the spy began his operations. He had access to the house, but the desk containing the coveted papers was locked. By rare good – or bad – fortune, the General had left his bunch of keys on a hook behind the door. Monsieur de Meinau possessed himself of them and opened the desk of the absent soldier. To his delight he found a mass of most important correspondence.

He tiptoed over to the door and locked it securely. After that he pulled down the blinds and started in to read the papers. It consumed several hours and at the end of that time he had discovered many things which he felt sure were important to Napoleon. The question now was whether to steal the papers or copy them. He finally decided on the latter course. There were two reasons for this. The first was that he could accomplish his purpose without exciting any suspicion and the second that the chief-of-staff, for whom he had come to hold a certain regard, would be held blameless.

He went at his work with a will. He used a cipher of his own which was a sort of shorthand, and long before the sun went down he had filled his memorandum books with most valuable information. Just as he finished there came a loud rapping at the door. He was startled, but not seriously disturbed. He concealed his notebook, locked the desk, placed the keys where he had found them, and then hastily undressed. A couch was in the corner of the room, and he threw himself on it. In the meantime the knocking had become more pronounced. He arose and opened the door, presenting a sleepy and dishevelled appearance to the man at the door. It proved to be, as he had expected, the chief-of-staff, returned from his tour of inspection. Monsieur de Meinau was all apologies.

"I am so sorry to have kept you waiting," he murmured, "but I was tired and I am a heavy sleeper."

The General was graciousness itself.

"No excuses are necessary," he insisted. "I regret having disturbed you. Please lie down again and take the rest I know you must need so badly."

After that speech it might be supposed that Monsieur de Meinau would relent. But not so. He had other uses for his victim. He had supper with him and late that night asked for a safe conduct to Vienna.

"I have to go after some information and it is too late to go to the Archduke. I am sure he would give it to me but I dislike disturbing him. Perhaps it is too much to ask from you?"

The chief-of-staff gave a gracious wave of the arm which might be taken to mean that everything he had was at the disposal of the spy. He said:

"It gives me great pleasure to serve you in this matter because in doing so I know that I am serving my country."

If Monsieur de Meinau had been capable of blushing he would have done so at that moment. But he merely sat there stolidly waiting while the General wrote the desired pass. When it was handed to him he put it in his wallet, bade his host an affectionate farewell and started off with the stolen correspondence.

He reached Vienna in safety and immediately reported to Napoleon, giving the Little Corporal not only the copies of the letters and papers, but also a great amount of verbal information. Napoleon already had his plans made for the campaign which was to end by placing his brother Jerome on the throne of Westphalia. The data given him by Monsieur de Meinau enabled him to dispose his forces still more advantageously. Also it placed the enemy at a tremendous disadvantage.

At this time there had been formed a new combination against France, consisting of England, Russia, Sweden, Saxony and Prussia. The contest began in 1806 with two thrilling battles, Jena and Auerstadt. They were fought on the same day. It was a crushing defeat for the Prussians, and Napoleon, already having possession of Vienna, now marched in triumph into Berlin. Well might he gloat over his triumph, for he had accomplished in a few hours what Austria, France and Russia had been unable to do in the Seven Years' War of the preceding century. And within a stone's throw of the Emperor and sharing with him the glories of this historic occasion was his faithful spy.

But the opposition, while dismayed, was not yet entirely vanquished. The Prussians gathered their scattered forces together and joining with the Russians made a final stand at Eylau. The battle there was fierce, but not decisive. A short time after this the French won the battle of Friedland, and then a treaty of peace was signed.

Napoleon gained precisely what he wanted. By the peace treaty Prussia gave up a large part of her territory. From a portion of it, lying west of the Elbe, he created the Kingdom of Westphalia. This was bestowed upon his brother Jerome, thus adding another kingdom to the group of states which he was accumulating and which – he thought in his colossal vanity – was to make him King of Kings. Monsieur de Meinau was present when Jerome was crowned, as was befitting for one who had risked his life in the cause of the king-maker.

In 1809 Monsieur de Meinau was given command of the Military Police of the French Army. From that date, although his field of Operations was increased, his personal exploits became less numerous. He did undertake one or two private missions for Napoleon, but for the most part his hours were fully occupied in directing the activities of others. That he was a busy man may be appreciated from the ceaseless labors of Napoleon. That remarkable man never rested and, needless to say, did not permit any one about him to rest. There came the seizure of the thrones of Portugal and Spain, the Peninsular War, the quarrel with the Pope, the battle of Wagram and then the divorce from

Josephine and the marriage to the Princess Marie Louise. In all of these stirring events the former Alsatian smuggler played his part.

Napoleon, while a hard taskmaster, was a liberal paymaster. Time and again his spy was given large sums of money, and what was quite as good, the opportunities of making money. But there was one thing he craved, and that was the cross of the Legion of Honor. He had been a soldier as well as a spy, and felt that this entitled him to the decoration. Familiar as he had been with the Man of Destiny, the spy did not have the courage to personally ask him for this favor. He confided his wish to General Savery, his original patron, who undertook to present the case to the Emperor. The great Napoleon had ideas of his own on this point. He fully appreciated the value of the services rendered by Schulmeister but when the decoration was demanded he gave an aggressive shake of the head.

"Money as much as you like," he cried, "but the cross – never!"

And the money poured into the outstretched hands of Monsieur de Meinau, but the decoration of the Legion of Honor remained ever beyond his reach. Presently the fortunes of Napoleon began to wane, and, appropriately enough the fortunes of his chief spy also waned. He became a comparatively poor man and went to spend the declining years of his life in the town of his birth. There Napoleon III called on him and talked of the great days that had gone before.

Sometime in the forties a Parisian visiting the Alsatian village met a little old man, dressed in black, and walking about with the aid of a cane. In spite of his great age he was nattily attired and the red rose in his buttonhole betokened the spirit of youth that dwelt within him. He was amiable and very, very gentle. This man was Louis Joseph Schulmeister, afterwards Monsieur de Meinau, Napoleon's chief spy, and the hero of a hundred thrilling escapes.

The good, it is said, die young; this amazing man lived to be eighty-two, and died in bed!

5

The strange mystery surrounding the betrayal of Captain Nathan Hale

Most Americans are fairly familiar with the story of the heroic sacrifice of Captain Nathan Hale, but none have yet ventured to remove the veil of mystery that hides the identity of the betrayer of the young patriot.

Who delivered Nathan Hale into the hands of his executioners? That is a question which has never been answered. Was it one of his own cousins who happened to be a Tory and a British sympathizer? That suspicion has been expressed and although it has been pushed aside by Benson J. Lossing the historian, he admits that he has not been able to obtain any data for or against this theory.

It is a notorious fact that the Tories were very numerous in and about New York, and there seems to be reason for believing that some of Hale's own family were in sympathy with their sycophantic sentiments. Could feelings of envy have entered into one of the saddest betrayals of American history? It is to be hoped not for the sake of our common humanity, and yet the popularity of Hale as he reached man's estate was likely to arouse the mean jealousy of those of a lower order of mentality.

Nathan Hale was a magnificent specimen of manhood. His physical and mental qualities were alike distinguished. He was graduated from Yale college with high honors and while there made a record as an athlete. He was almost six feet in height, perfectly proportioned, and, in the words of Dr Munson, was "the most manly man I have ever met." His chest was broad, his muscles firm; his face wore a most benign expression; his complexion was rosy; his eyes, light blue and beaming with intelligence; his hair soft and light brown and his speech low, sweet and musical. Is it any wonder that the girls of New Haven loved him and wept when they heard his fate?

Nathan Hale was engaged in teaching school at New London when the rumbles of the Revolution first began to disturb the placid life of that part of the country. On the day that American blood was first shed at Lexington a twilight town meeting was called and Nathan Hale was one of the speakers. He called upon the people to act at once and to act in a manner that could not be misunderstood.

"Let us march immediately," he cried with all of the passionate ardor of youth, "and let us never lay down our arms until we have obtained our independence."

As a proof of both his consistency and his patriotism, Hale immediately enrolled himself as a volunteer. The following morning he bade good-by to his pupils and departed for Cambridge. Before long he had been formally enlisted as a lieutenant of a company in a regiment commanded by Colonel Charles Webb, and late in September of that year marched with his regiment to Cambridge and participated in the siege of Boston. Within three months he had been commissioned as a captain because of vigilance and bravery. The British were driven from Boston in the spring of the following year, and soon after that the Americans proceeded to New York. His earnestness in the cause was proven when he surrendered his own pay to his men in the endeavor to have them prolong their term of service, which had already expired.

Even at this early stage of his military career he covered himself with glory by performing what proved to be one of the most daring feats of the Revolution. A British sloop laden with provisions was anchored in the East River under the protection of the guns of a man-of-war called the Asia. Hale went to General Heath and obtained permission to attempt the capture of the supply vessel. With a few dozen picked men as resolute as himself, he embarked in a small boat at midnight and reached the side of the sloop unobserved by the sentinel. The young New Englander followed by his men sprang aboard the vessel, secured the sentinel, confined the crew below the hatches, raised the boat's anchor and took her into the wharf just at the dawn of day. It was a dashing adventure and it was successful. He was the hero of the hour, especially among his fellow Americans, when the supplies were distributed among them. For many months after this he continued the routine work of a captain in the

Revolutionary Army, and it was not until the 7th of September that he was called upon to take part in the thrilling exploit which was to end in such a disastrous and tragic manner. Washington had called a council of war to decide whether he should defend or abandon New York. He had already asked Congress this important question and he was answered by a resolution that in case he should find it necessary to quit New York he should have special care taken that no damage be done to the city. As a result of this he resolved to remain and defend the city.

General Washington had at this time made his headquarters at the house of Robert Murray. The position of his army was exceedingly perilous, ships of war having already passed up the East River. Scouts reported great activity among the British troops, but they were unable, after great efforts, to gain any intelligent idea of the intentions of the enemy. Yet Washington knew that it was most essential that he should have this information. He wrote to General Heath, then staying at Kings Bridge.

"As everything in a manner depends upon intelligence of the enemy's motions, I do most earnestly entreat you and General Clinton to exert yourselves to accomplish this most desirable thing. Leave no stone unturned nor do not stick at expense to bring this to pass, as I was never more uneasy than on account of my want of knowledge on this score. Keep a constant lookout with good glasses on some commanding heights that look well on to the other shore."

What Washington desired to know more than anything else was whether the British would make a direct attack upon the city, and if they did whether they intended to land upon the island above the city or Morrisania, beyond the Harlem River. The general in his perplexity called another council of war at Murray's. At this conference it was resolved to send some courageous and competent person in disguise into the British camps on Long Island. The person needed was one skilled in military and scientific knowledge and a good draftsman – in short a man on whose judgment and fidelity they could absolutely depend. In this emergency Washington sent for Lieutenant Colonel Noulton and told him just what he wanted. In response Noulton summoned a number of officers to a conference at his quarters and in the name of the commander-in-chief called for volunteers. They were taken by surprise. There was a general reluctance to engage in the work of a spy. For a time it looked as if it would be impossible to obtain a man for the service, but at the last moment a young soldier who had been ill entered the room and learning the nature of the request called out:

"I will undertake the work."

It was Captain Nathan Hale. Everybody was amazed, not the least among them being Lieutenant Colonel Noulton. Some of the others, who knew and loved Hale, privately endeavored to persuade him to reconsider his decision. They pointed out his hopes for the future and explained the ignominy and death to which he might be exposed. One of his dearest friends, William Hull, who was afterwards a general in the War of 1812, and who was a member of his company and had been his classmate at college, was especially fervid in trying to turn him from the perilous task, but Hale had made up his mind and would not change it. He said with great warmth:

"Gentlemen, I am satisfied that I owe to my country the accomplishment of an object so important and so much desired by the commander of her armies, and I know of no mode of obtaining the information except by assuming a disguise and passing into the enemy's camp. I am fully sensible of the consequences of discovery and capture in such circumstances, but for a year I have been attached to the army and have not rendered any material service, while receiving a compensation for which I made no return. Yet I am not influenced by any expectation of promotion or pecuniary reward. I wish to be useful; and every kind of service necessary for the public good becomes honorable by being necessary. If the exigencies of my country demand a peculiar service its claims to the performance of that service are imperious."

These words, thrilling with their patriotism, silenced the objections of his fellow soldiers. That very afternoon in company with Noulton he appeared before Washington and received instructions concerning his mission. He was provided with the necessary authority and also given a general order to the owners of all American vessels to convey him to any point on Long Island which he might designate.

He left the camp on Harlem Heights that night accompanied by Sergeant Stephen Hempstead. With him also was his servant, Ansel Wright. It was not until they had reached Norwalk, fifty miles from New York, that they found a safe place to cross the Sound. Here Hale exchanged his regimentals for citizen's dress of brown cloth and a broad brimmed round hat. He directed his two companions to remain there until his return and also deposited with Hempstead his uniform and his military commission. Hale crossed the Sound to Huntingdon Bay where he landed disguised in the character of schoolmaster and Royalist who was disgusted with the Rebel forces. He entered the British camps in this disguise and was received with much enthusiasm by the Redcoats, who accepted him as an ally. It is known that he visited all the British camps on Long Island and made observations openly; that he passed over from Brooklyn to New York City and that he gathered considerable information concerning the condition of the British army at that place. So far he had been entirely successful in his mission.

On his return he safely reached the point on the Long Island shore where he had first landed, and he prepared to re-cross the Sound at Norwalk the first thing in the following morning. He wore shoes with loose inner soles and between the soles he had concealed the drawings he made of the fortifications and also other memoranda written in Latin on thin paper. Perfectly satisfied that he was safe from harm and filled with the thought that his mission had ended successfully, he calmly awaited the coming of daylight. His attention was attracted by the proximity of an inn known as "The Cedars." This place was managed by a widow who was a staunch Loyalist. It was well known as the resort of the Tories in that part of the country. Hale was familiar with these facts, but was not disturbed at the thought of any personal danger.

The light in the window of "The Cedars" attracted him. It was necessary that he should have refreshments and lodgings.

He felt perfectly safe now, considering that he was far away from the danger zone, and besides felt that his simple attire would protect him from prying eyes. Accordingly he strolled into the tavern and secured a room for the night. After that he went to the main room and ordered supper. The place was fairly crowded and the entrance of Hale apparently attracted no attention.

He took his ease, supping leisurely and listening with interest to the gossip of the loungers about the room. "The Cedars" was notoriously a resort for Tories and the young American was forced to listen to some conversation which he surely did not relish. But he had a sense of humor as well as a philosophy of his own and the blatant talk of the so-called Royalists did not disturb the serenity of his disposition. Indeed, there is reason to believe that the romantic side of the young man was attracted by the novelty of the situation. "The Cedars" was a quaint old inn. The customary shingle, offering refreshments for "man and beast" swung outside in the wind; mine host with a long white apron served beer in great stone mugs, and the patrons of the place sprawled about the tables smoking long stemmed pipes. They talked of war and they talked of spies, little thinking that an American officer who was just finishing an important mission was listening to all they had to say.

In the midst of the hub-bub a stranger entered the room. He caught one glance of Nathan Hale and then turned his face with the suddenness of one who has made a startling discovery. The next moment Hale had looked up, but too late to get a good view of the man's face. He caught the merest glance of the guilty countenance, and from that moment his mind was haunted with a resemblance which it was impossible to fix with any certainty. The newcomer was in civilian's dress. He wore his hair long and was square-shouldered. He spoke to no one and disappeared as silently as he had entered.

There can be no doubt that he is the man who betrayed Hale to the British. But there has always been real doubt concerning his identity. It is hinted that Hale himself said that the fellow resembled a distant cousin. But there is nothing on record to prove this disagreeable suspicion. Indeed, from that moment, there seems to have been an attempt to conceal all of the facts concerning Hale's dramatic arrest and tragic death. Can this have been part of the plan to protect the informer? Over one hundred and forty years have passed since then and history still asks the name of the man who entered "The Cedars" on that fateful night in September, 1775.

Nathan Hale spent the night at this tavern, and at daylight the next morning he went out to search for the boat that was to convey him to the other side of the Sound. To his immense satisfaction he saw a craft moving towards the shore with several men in it. He had not the least doubt but that they were his friends and he hastened to the beach in order to meet it. As the boat touched the shore a half dozen British marines jumped out and surrounded him. He turned as if to run when a harsh voice exclaimed:

"Surrender instantly, or you die!"

Too late he realized that he had walked into a trap. He saw six men standing there erect with muskets levelled at his heart. It was folly to struggle. He was seized, taken into the barge and conveyed to the British guardship Halifax. His captors stripped and searched him and found the evidence of his mission concealed between the soles of his shoes. The unfortunate American was taken in one of the boats of the Halifax to General Howe's headquarters, which were then in the mansion of James Beekman at Mount Pleasant. This place contained among other things a great greenhouse filled with shrubbery and plants. In this greenhouse Hale was confined under a strong guard on the night of September 21. The following morning he was taken before Howe, who, without the formality of a trial, condemned him to be hung. He was delivered into the custody of William Cunningham with orders that he should be executed before sunrise the following day.

History informs us that when Hale was taken before Howe he frankly acknowledged the purpose of his mission.

"I was present at the interview," wrote a British officer, "and I observed that the frankness, the manly bearing and the evident disinterested patriotism of the young prisoner touched a tender cord in General Howe's nature; but the stern rules of war concerning such offenses would not allow him to exercise even pity."

It was on a Sunday morning that Nathan Hale was marched to the place of execution, which was in the vicinity of what is now East Broadway and Market Street. He was escorted by a file of soldiers and was permitted to sit in a tent while waiting for the necessary preparations for his death. The young patriot asked for a chaplain but his request was brutally denied. He asked for a Bible, but this also was refused. It was only at the solicitation of a young officer in whose tent Hale sat that he was allowed to write brief letters to his mother, sisters and the young girl to whom he was betrothed. She was Alice Adams, a native of Canterbury, Connecticut, and distinguished both for her intelligence and personal beauty. Who could imagine the feelings that filled the young patriot as he penned his final words to the girl who was pledged to be his wife.

But imagine the scene a moment later when these tender epistles were handed to Cunningham. That officer read them with growing anger. He became furious as he realized the noble spirit which breathed in every word. He resolved that they should not be given to the world, and with an oath tore them into bits before the face of his victim. It was twilight on that beautiful September morning when Hale was led to his execution. The gallows was the limb of an apple tree in Colonel Rutger's orchard. The young martyr was asked if he had anything to say. He turned to his executioner and in a calm clear voice said:

"I only regret that I have but one life to lose for my country."

NATHAN HALE

His body was buried near the spot where he died and a British officer was sent to acquaint Washington with the fate of his young messenger. A rude stone placed by the side of the grave of his father in the burial ground of the Congregational Church in his native town for many years revealed to passersby the fact that it was "In Commemoration of Nathan Hale, Esquire, a Captain in the Army of the United States, who was Born June Sixth, 1755, and Received the First Honors of Yale College, September 17,

1773, and Resigned His Life a Sacrifice to His Country's Liberty at New York, September 22, 1776, Age Twenty-two."

Sixty years ago, long before there was a monument to the memory of Hale, George Gibbs, librarian of the New York Historical Society, wrote this epitaph, which is worthy of preservation:

Stranger, beneath this stone
Lies the dust of
A spy,
Who perished upon the gibbet;
Yet
The storied marbles of the great,
The shrines of heroes,
Entombed one not more worthy of
Honor
Than him who here
Sleeps his last sleep.
Nations
Bow with reverence before the dust
Of him who dies
A glorious death,
Urged on by the sound of the
Trumpet
And the shouts of
Admiring thousands
But what reverence, what honor,
Is not due to one,

Who for his country encountered
Even an infamous death,
Soothed by no sympathy,
Animated by no praise!

The simple narrative of Nathan Hale's life and death effectively disposes of the tradition that he undertook his perilous mission reluctantly or that he had any scruples about essaying the role of a spy. He regarded that task as part of the day's work – an unpleasant part to be sure, but one of the things that had to be cheerfully undertaken in the line of duty.

But there is one phase of the tragic business that is shrouded in mystery and it is the story of his betrayal. Who was the strange man in "The Cedars"? Was he a cousin? Was he a Tory? Do the descendants of that man still live in New York City and what must their feelings be when they read the inscription upon the monument to the young patriot and martyr?

Until these questions have been answered and until this mystery has been made clear the story of Nathan Hale will be incomplete.

6

Major Le Caron and the Fenian Invasion of Canada

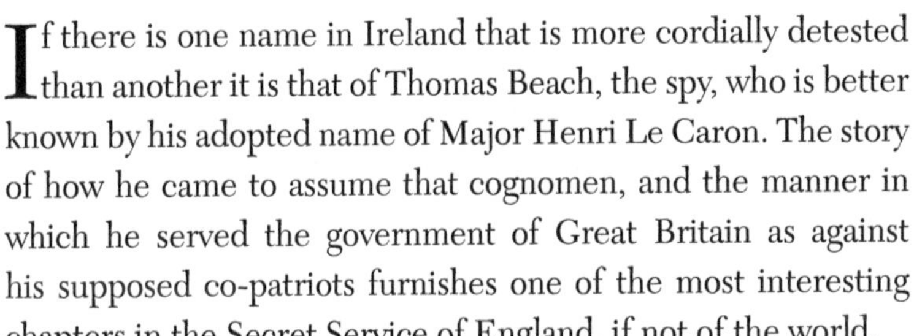

If there is one name in Ireland that is more cordially detested than another it is that of Thomas Beach, the spy, who is better known by his adopted name of Major Henri Le Caron. The story of how he came to assume that cognomen, and the manner in which he served the government of Great Britain as against his supposed co-patriots furnishes one of the most interesting chapters in the Secret Service of England, if not of the world.

Beach defends his work on the ground that when he was first brought into contact with Fenianism he had no ulterior motive in mind and that no material consideration prompted him to work against the men who hoped to bring about the freedom of Ireland by the spectacular invasion of Canada. He says that he was forced by a variety of circumstances to play a part he had never sought, but he insists that he did nothing to be ashamed of and has never felt any regret for the manner in which he served England. He says that there is no truth in the popular belief which credited him with receiving fabulous payments and frequent rewards. He admits that there was ever-present danger and constantly recurring difficulties, but very scant recompense from the Government for which he risked so much.

Beach was born in England, but came to the United States just about the time of the beginning of the Civil War and enlisted in the Union Army – in the 8th Pennsylvanian Reserves. But in enlisting he took on himself a new name and a new nationality. One reason he gives for this was his desire to avoid giving his parents anxiety. Also he thought it would be "a good joke." Be that as it may, he was put down on the books of his company as Henri Le Caron and his home as France. He served through the greater part of the war, and after it was over became connected with the Grand Army of the Republic, holding among other positions those of Vice Commander and Post Surgeon, with the rank of major.

MAJOR LE CARON (Thomas Beach)

So from that time until the end of the chapter he was known as Major Le Caron, and he says that this afforded him an effective disguise through which he was enabled to keep the English authorities informed of the Irish movements on this side of the Atlantic.

It was through an Irishman named O'Neill that Le Caron became connected with the Fenian movement. He wrote home at intervals and he says that the information which was thus informally given to his family was by them taken to the Home Secretary in London, and in the course of time Le Caron became a regularly paid spy in the Secret Service. The consequences of this was that the proposed invasion of Canada was well known to the English and Canadian officials long before it occurred. The first invasion, with which Le Caron does not seem to have been personally connected occurred on the morning of June 1, 1866. For six months before that time active preparations were in progress. During the spring of the year many companies of soldiers, armed and uniformed, were being drilled in a number of cities in the United States. Thousands of stands of arms and millions of rounds of ammunition had been purchased and located at different points along the Canadian border.

The relations between the United States and England were not very cordial at that time because of the attitude of England during the Civil War, and as a consequence the proposed invasion, if it was not encouraged, was not greatly discouraged in this country. The attempt, however, proved a failure. The Fenians were defeated and driven out of Canada. Sixty of them were killed and more than two hundred taken prisoners. It was the natural result that is to be looked for when a volunteer force goes against a well trained army. Under the command of General John O'Neill 800 Irish patriots were towed across the Niagara River to a point on the Canadian side called Waterloo. At four o'clock in the morning the Irish flag was planted on British soil by Colonel Owen Starr, and from thence the patriots marched to and captured Fort Erie, containing a detachment of the Welland Battery.

The effect of the news of this first victory was electrical in the United States. Thousands who had hesitated about joining the movement were now willing and anxious to enlist. The Canadian Government, and Le Caron in his official reports to London endeavored to belittle this initial triumph, but they felt very much chagrined just the same. However, the Irish victory was short-lived. As soon as the news of the capture of Fort Erie spread to Toronto, the 22nd Battalion of Volunteers of that city hastened to the rescue, and at Ridgeway a bloody battle occurred between the opposing forces. The invaders were driven back to Fort Erie and later were taken as prisoners by the United States battleship Michigan.

The news of the temporary victory had a wonderful effect in the United States. By the 7th of June not less than 30,000 men had assembled in and around Buffalo, prepared to fight if it was deemed desirable. But the defeat of the detachment that had actually entered Canada, and the issuance of a neutrality proclamation by President Andrew Johnson ended the war for the time being. The prisoners were released on their own recognizance and sent home by the United States authorities. The arms seized by the American Government were returned to the Fenian organization, and if Dame Rumor is not a falsifier, were used for a second invasion of Canada four years later.

In 1869 Le Caron was so intimate with his Fenian friends that he was made an inspector general of the Irish Republican Army. After that he was assistant adjutant general with the rank of colonel, and his new position enabled him not only to become possessed of the originals of many important documents and plans of proposed campaigns, but also specimens of the Fenian army commissions which he promptly conveyed to the officials of the Canadian Government. In this work he was assisted by a number of officials from Canada. Speaking of this, he says:

"Successful as I was in avoiding detection through all this work, those assisting me in my secret service capacity were not always destined to share in my good luck. This has been particularly the case on one occasion. I was at the time shipping arms at Malone, N. Y., and attended on behalf of the Canadian Government by one of the staff men placed at my disposal for the purpose of immediate communication and the transit of any documents requiring secrecy and dispatch as well as for personal protection should such prove necessary. This man, John C. Rose, was one of the most faithful and trusted servants of the Canadian administration, and for months he followed me along the whole border.

"Though stopping at the same hotels and in constant communication with me, no suspicion was aroused until his identity was accidentally disclosed by a visitor from the seat of government to one of the Fenians located at Malone. Men were immediately set to watch him without my knowledge, and the fact of his being found always in my wake on my visits to and from several towns led to the belief that he was spying upon my actions. A few nights after this poor Rose on his return from sending a dispatch from the post office, was waylaid, robbed and brutally beaten, and subsequently brought back to the hotel in as sorry a plight as I ever saw."

In the meantime, in the winter of 1869, the Fenian Senate announced the completion of the arrangements for the invasion of Canada, and early in February the following year circulars were sent out to the military officers of the Fenian Brotherhood, instructing them to prepare for the proposed campaign. Those Brothers whose business or family duties prevented them from getting their commands in readiness for active and immediate service were requested to forward their resignations at once and at the same time send on the names of persons suitable to take their places. They were told to ascertain and report how many of their own men could furnish their own transportation, and in the meantime to try and persuade all of them to save enough for that purpose.

On Saturday, April 22, 1870, General O'Neill and Le Caron left Buffalo for St. Albans, the general being filled with enthusiasm over the belief that the Canadians would be taken entirely by surprise, and Le Caron laughing in his sleeve at the thought of how his companion would be fooled. O'Neill's plan was to get across the boundary line without delay and then to entrench himself at a point where his soldiers would form the nucleus around which a large army and unlimited support would rally from the United States. Buffalo, Malone, and Franklin were the three points from which attacks were to be made. O'Neill expected 1,000 men to meet him at Franklin, on the night of April 25, 1870. Only a quarter of that number presented themselves, and by the following morning not more than 500 had mustered. Every hour's delay added to the danger of failure and collapse. All this time Le Caron was busy sending messages across the border carrying full details as to the time the Fenians would leave Franklin, the exact points at which they would cross the border, their numbers, and the places of their contemplated operation.

On April 26 O'Neill left the Franklin Hotel to place himself at the head of the Fenian Army. Hubbard's Farm, the Fenian camp and rendezvous, was about half a mile from Franklin, and here all of the available soldiers had been mustered. Arranging them in line, O'Neill, according to Le Caron's narrative, addressed them as follows:

"Soldiers, this is the advance guard of the Irish-American army for the liberation of Ireland from the yoke of the oppressor. For the sake of your own country you enter that of the enemy. The eyes of your countrymen are upon you. Forward, march!"

Following this harangue they started off on their expedition with O'Neill at their head. Before leaving, O'Neill instructed Le Caron to bring to his support on their arrival a party of 400 men who were coming from St. Albans. The men marched with a certain amount of military precision for all of them had received some degree of military training. There is no doubt of the patriotic feelings that filled their hearts. In spite of the lack of uniformity, and possibly because of it, the scene was picturesque. Here and there a Fenian coat with its green and gray faced with gold sparkled in contrast with the civilian clothing and the more somber garb of the others.

Finally the volunteers reached a little wooden bridge and deployed as skirmishers in close order, advancing with fixed bayonets and cheering wildly. Not a soldier appeared to dispute their way, but the dark Canadian trees hid from their view the ambushed Canadian volunteers, who were only awaiting the signal to spring out upon the unsuspecting invaders.

All this time Le Caron, who had spent years of intimate association with many of the Irishmen and who was regarded as their friend and confidant, stood upon the hilltop to watch the inevitable slaughter. They advanced a few yards farther, and on their startled ears came the whistling sound of many bullets from the rifles of the ambushed Canadians as they poured a deadly volley straight into their ranks.

Little remains to be told. There was fierce fighting and terrible bloodshed, but the invaders were overcome by superior numbers and well disciplined troops. Finally they were forced to retreat up to the hill where Le Caron stood, still under the fire of their adversaries and leaving their dead to be subsequently buried by the Canadians.

Seeing that all was over, for the time at least, the spy had hurried off to the point where the St. Albans contingent had arrived and were forming. He actually took part in this ceremony, and while engaged in superintending it he was afforded, as he says, practical evidence of the termination of O'Neill's part in the fight. While he was standing in the middle of the road where the men were forming into line, he was startled by the cry:

"Clear the road, clear the road!"

He was almost knocked down by a team of horses pulling a covered carriage, and as the conveyance flashed by him he caught through the carriage window a hurried glimpse of the dejected face of General O'Neill, who was seated between two men. He said in speaking of this that he might have given the command to shoot the horses as they turned an adjacent corner, but it was no part of his purpose to restore O'Neill to his command.

It became known later that O'Neill was in the custody of the United States Marshal, General Foster, who, acting under instructions from Washington, had arrived on the scene of the battle immediately after Le Caron left and arrested O'Neill on the charge of breaking the neutrality laws. O'Neill, who was in the company of his comrades, refused to surrender and threatened force, but when General Foster placed a revolver at his head he succumbed.

Late that afternoon when the news of O'Neill's arrest became known, a council of war was held, presided over by John Boyle O'Reilly. On the following morning General Spear, the secretary of war of the Fenian Brotherhood, arrived at St. Albans and tried to do something practical in the way of continuing the invasion. He pleaded with Le Caron to supply him with 400 or 500 stands of arms and ammunition within the next twenty-four hours, but the spy felt that it would not do for him to allow further operations, and so he said that it would be impossible to grant the demands under the condition of affairs then prevailing. Thousands of Canadian troops had arrived on the border and were making the position of the Irish volunteers more precarious every moment.

Fortunately for Le Caron, the appearance of United States troops in the vicinity put any further attempt at war operations out of the question, for in order to avoid arrest for a breach of the neutrality laws the Fenians were compelled to disappear. The spy left with them and hurried to Malone and found a similar state of affairs prevailing there, although the arrest of O'Neill and the anticipated appearance of United States troops filled the invaders with dismay.

Le Caron was elated with his success and anxious to report himself at the Canadian headquarters without delay. He knew, however, that it would not be safe for him to go direct to Ottawa so he traveled in a roundabout way. One night he stopped with the Commissioner of the Quebec police, and the following morning took a train for Ottawa. Before this journey was concluded he found that he had been altogether too premature in his self congratulations, because that journey brought him closer to discovery than he had ever been before.

The incident which threatened to deprive him of his usefulness as a spy occurred at Cornwall where there was the usual half hour's delay for dinner. He was in the midst of his meal, enjoying it with great zest in spite of the fact that his work as a spy had sent hundreds of men to their death, when two men stopped and gazed at him with unusual interest. One of them was tall and very military in his manner, and the other had on clerical attire. As Le Caron ceased eating he heard the clerical looking one say as he pointed his finger in his direction:

"That is the man!"

Advancing, the tall man, who subsequently turned out to be the Mayor of Cornwall, said with a Scotch accent:

"You are my prisoner!"

These words were accompanied with a strong grasp of the hand on the shoulder of the suspected one. He imagined there was some mistake, and laughed as he turned around to resume his dinner, but the Scotchman gave an added squeeze to his arm as he solemnly repeated the words:

"You are my prisoner, and you must go with me at once."

It turned out later that the ministerial looking person was a wandering preacher who happened to be in the vicinity of

Malone when Le Caron was loading arms there and he had been pointed out to him as the leading Fenian agent. The preacher's memory was a very good one, and he immediately recognized the spy when he met him again.

It was a serious condition of affairs for Le Caron, but still he could not entirely comprehend what it all meant, and he said:

"Will not you let me finish my dinner?"

"No," was the sharp reply, "you have got to come at once."

"For what reason am I arrested?" asked Le Caron.

"You are a Fenian," was the indignant reply, and then for the first time the spy noticed that the crowd in the room was beginning to show signs of anger and indignation toward him.

He was hurried out by his captors and taken to a room adjoining the ticket office, where a demand was made on him for his luggage and keys with everything on his person. He had with him documents which would reveal everything if they were made public. His position was dangerous, as he puts it "distinctly dangerous."

In this emergency he asked the Mayor for a few minutes' private conversation, and it was accorded him. They went inside the ticket office and Le Caron told him the exact situation. It was true, he admitted, that he had been working with the Fenians, but he was also a Government agent. In fact he was a British spy who had been keeping the Canadian officials informed of the details of the proposed invasion. He said that he was then on his way to Ottawa to see Judge McMicken. He said that to delay or expose him would mean serious difficulty to the Government.

His manner must have impressed the Mayor, for he decided to send him on to Ottawa in charge of an escort with instructions to find out from Judge McMicken whether his story was to be believed. The details of Le Caron's arrest as a Fenian quickly spread amongst his fellow passengers and the reception he received along the journey was not very agreeable, so for safety's sake the lieutenant transferred him to the care of a sergeant and two other soldiers. The carriage in which they traveled was the sole point of attraction in the train, and the Canadians, crowding around this carriage, hissed and hooted him, while their cries of "Hang him! Lynch him!" gave him a very uncomfortable idea of what would happen if he were left alone amongst them.

On reaching Prescott junction Le Caron found the news of his capture had preceded him and created such a sensation that a special correspondent of the Toronto Globe had traveled to meet him in order to find out who and what he was and everything about him. The spy of course refused to have anything to say. When the party arrived at Ottawa a representative of Judge McMicken was waiting for him at the station. He was conveyed to the police station without delay, and there the judge heard the details of his capture and received possession of his person and gave a formal receipt for his custody. After the guard left the judge listened to the recital of the spy and arranged that his identity should not become public. He also supplied him with needful funds to leave Canada. This came in the form of a check and it was necessary to have someone cash it. This was done at one of the clubs in Ottawa and the amount of the check – $350.00 – caused the club porter to speak of it to some of his friends. This porter knew that Le Caron was the Fenian prisoner and he let out the secret a little later. It became public property and the

Canadian press published the fact that an important Fenian had been in Ottawa immediately after the raid and received a large sum of money from a Government official with whom he was in communication, adding that the Fenians must have been nicely duped all through.

Le Caron was very much disturbed by this publication. It was bringing danger very close to him, and yet strange as it may appear, suspicion did not rest upon him in connection with the newspaper story. He drove from Ottawa in the night and got safely home, not being troubled afterwards by any of the events of that fateful invasion into Canada.

Le Caron studied medicine after that and subsequently became connected with the Clan-na-Gael. He became one of the members of the military board of organization and in that capacity continued to send information to his friends at Scotland Yard. While he was in this organization he became acquainted with many of its leading members who believed that he was really a friend of Ireland and who never suspected that he was connected with the British Government and was regularly receiving compensation for the information which he sent from time to time to the home office in London.

Le Caron continued to serve as an English spy for nearly twenty years after the Fenian invasion of Canada. His part in that affair – or at least the part he played in keeping the Canadian and English governments informed of the movements of the Irish patriots – was never suspected by the men with whom he was associated and with whom he lived on such intimate terms. He was in constant communication with Mr. Anderson, the head of

Scotland Yard, and his letters to that official, if gathered together, would make a volume in themselves. On one occasion when he was leaving America for a trip abroad he was entrusted with letters to Patrick Egan and other Irish leaders. He met Egan in Paris, and spent weeks with him in visiting places of interest in the French capital. They attended the theater together and dined at various restaurants in company, and Le Caron proudly boasts that he never had to spend a penny, because Egan insisted upon being the host at their various entertainments.

But it was when the famous suit of Parnell against the London Times was tried that the spy was at last revealed in his true light. He says of that event:

"On Tuesday morning, the 5th of February, 1889, the curtain was rung up, and throwing aside the mask forever, I stepped into the witness box and came out in my true colors, as an Englishman, proud of his country, and in no sense ashamed of his record in her services."

His one complaint was that he had been treated badly in the matter of his pay by the British Government. He said that "the miserable pittance doled out for the purpose of fighting the Clan-na-Gael becomes perfectly ludicrous" in the light of the service he was called on to perform.

It all depends upon the way in which the business is regarded, and there are still a great many persons that will resent the effort of Thomas Beach, or Major Henri Le Caron, to place a halo about his head.

7

How Emma Edmonds penetrated the Confederate lines

This is a leaf from the life of an extraordinary woman who served as a nurse and a spy in the Union army during the Civil War in the United States, and who was a pronounced success in both capacities. Few women that have passed through such thrilling adventures are so little known to fame, yet if the patient seeker be willing to spare the time and the labor he may find in the files of the War Department at Washington reports in her handwriting which had a material influence upon more than one battle during the four years of the war.

Emma Edmonds was an adopted American. She was born and educated in the province of New Brunswick, but came to the United States at an early age. She was passing through New York on her way to her future home in New England when the newspapers appeared on the street with the announcement of the fall of Fort Sumter, and President Lincoln's call for seventy-five thousand men. That happening changed the entire course of her life. Ten days later she had been enrolled as a field nurse in the Union army, and was in Washington waiting to be detailed for duty.

The first assignment came sooner than was expected. Almost before she knew it she was in the thick of the work that followed the battle of Manassas. She spent three hours with other nurses in caring for the needs of the men – even while the battle was in progress. Presently the enemy made a desperate charge on the Union troops, driving them back and taking possession of the spring from which they obtained their water. The chaplain's horse was shot from under him and bled to death in a little while. Not long afterwards Colonel Cameron, brother of the Secretary of War, came dashing along the line shouting:

"Come on, boys, they're in full retreat!"

The words had scarcely been uttered when he fell, pierced to the heart by a bullet. It was mortal and all that the nurse could do was to fold his arms, close his eyes and leave him in the cold embrace of death. And all the while the battle raged about them. This was but one of a score of incidents that prepared a frail woman for the breath-taking career which she was to follow during the four years of the Civil War – incidents which are more thrilling than those to be found in the pages of the most exciting fiction.

All of this was preliminary to Emma Edmonds' work as a spy. One morning a detachment of the Thirty-seventh New York Regiment that had been sent out on scouting duty returned with several prisoners and the statement that one of the Federal spies had been captured and executed. There was regret, not alone over the death of the man, but also because a valuable soldier had been lost to the United States Secret Service. Incidentally it brought the opportunity for which the fearless woman had been waiting. She was told that she might have the opportunity of becoming a spy if she fully realized the danger and the responsibility that was attached to the post. She considered it carefully and said that if appointed she would accept and do the best she knew how for the Government.

Her name was sent to headquarters, and she was soon summoned to appear there herself. She was questioned and cross-questioned at some length; she was examined at length as to her knowledge of firearms, and finally the oath of allegiance was administered and she became a regular commissioned spy for the Federal army. It was at once decided that she should adopt a disguise and attempt to penetrate the Confederate lines.

In the first place she purchased a suit of contraband clothing, real plantation style such as the male negroes wore, and then went to a barber and had her hair sheared close to her head. After that, by the use of stains and dyes she colored her face, and then she was ready for business. It might be well to state, at this stage of the narrative, that Emma Edmonds while in the secret service penetrated the enemy's lines, in various disguises, no less than eleven times; always with complete success and without detection.

She started on her first expedition toward the Confederate capitol with the greatest confidence imaginable. With a few hard crackers in her pocket and her revolver loaded and capped she began the journey on foot, and without a blanket or any other kind of baggage that might excite suspicion. At half-past nine o'clock at night she passed the outer picket line of the Union army and at twelve o'clock was within the Confederate lines without once being halted by a sentinel. Once she passed within ten rods of a Confederate picket without being detected.

As soon as she had gone a safe distance from the picket lines she lay down and rested until morning. The night was chilly and the ground damp and she passed the weary hours in fear and trembling. The first thing in the morning she met a party of negroes carrying hot coffee and provisions to the Confederate pickets. This was most fortunate for she made their acquaintance, and after securing a hot breakfast she marched into Yorktown with them without eliciting the slightest suspicion. The negroes went to work at once on fortifications that were being erected, and the spy was left by herself. But an officer seeing her a few minutes later turned to an overseer and said:

"Take that black rascal and set him to work, and if he don't work well tie him up and give him twenty lashes."

So saying he rode away, and the disguised one was conducted to a breastwork which was in course of erection and where there were about a hundred negroes at work. She was soon furnished with a pick and shovel and a wheelbarrow and put to work. It was hard – hard enough for the strongest man, but with occasional assistance from some kind-hearted darky she managed to do her part. All day long she worked in this manner until her hands were blistered and her back nearly broken. When night came she was released from her toil and was free to go where she pleased. She made good use of her liberty. She wandered about the place and made out a brief report of the mounted guns she found in her ramble around the fort. There were fifteen three-inch rifle cannon, eighteen four and a half inch rifle cannon, twenty-nine thirty-two pounders, twenty-three eight-inch Columbiads, eleven nine-inch Dalgrens, thirteen ten-inch Columbiads, fourteen ten-inch mortars and seven eight-inch siege howitzers.

This capitulation must sound strange to those acquainted with present-day methods of warfare, but it was all very important to the spy, who made out her list with the greatest care. After that she made a rough sketch of the outer works, and placing the precious papers under the inner sole of her contraband shoe she returned to the negro quarters. She did not want to stay with them, but she did wish to find some one among them who would change places with her on the following day. She was fortunate in discovering a lad of about her own size who was engaged in carrying water to the troops. He said he would take her place next day and he thought he could find a friend to do the same thing the following day, for which evidence of brotherly kindness the female spy offered him $5.00 in greenbacks, which, he said, was more money than he had ever seen in all of his life before. By this arrangement Miss Edmonds escaped the scrutiny of the overseer, who might have detected her disguise.

The second day in the Confederate service was pleasanter than the first. She had only to supply one brigade with water, which did not require much energy, for the day was cool and the well not far distant. As a result of this she had an opportunity of lounging among the soldiers and of hearing important steps discussed. In this way she learned the number of reinforcements which had arrived from different places and also had the pleasure of seeing General Lee, who came there to consult with other Confederates. It was whispered among the men that he had been telegraphed to for the purpose of inspecting the fortifications, as he was the best engineer in the Confederacy and that he had pronounced it impossible to hold Yorktown after McClellan opened his siege guns upon it. General Johnson was hourly expected with a force at his command, and including all, the Confederates estimated their force in and around Yorktown at 150,000 men.

When General Johnson arrived a council of war was held. Soon after that the report began to circulate that the town was to be evacuated. It was at this stage of the game that Miss Edmonds saw a man who had been coming into the Federal camp as a peddler of newspapers and stationery, and now here he was giving the Confederates a full description of the Union camp and the Union forces. She watched him closely and discovered him displaying a map of the entire works of McClellan's position.

Miss Edmonds decided that it was of the utmost importance for her to leave the camp of the enemy and carry the information she possessed to the Union headquarters. The important thing now was to leave without being detected. On the evening of the third day from the time she entered the camp of the enemy she was sent in company with colored men to carry supper to the outer picket posts. This was just what she hoped and wished for. During the day she had provided herself with a canteen of whisky. Some of the men on picket duty were colored and others were white, but calling them to her side she spread before them corn cake and added to that a moderate amount of whisky for dessert. While they were thus engaged minnie balls were whistling around their heads, for the picket lines of the two armies were not more than half a mile distant from each other.

Not long after nightfall an officer came riding along the lines, and seeing the spy there, wanted to know his business. One of the darkies replied that she had helped to carry out their supper and was waiting until the Yankees stopped firing before she started back. Turning to the disguised one, he said:

"You come along with me. I'll see that you have something to occupy your mind."

Miss Edmonds did as she was ordered and they went back the way he had come until they had gone about fifty rods, then halting in front of a petty officer he said:

"Put this fellow on the post where that man was shot – and see that he stays there until I return."

So the spy was conducted a few rods farther and then a rifle put in her hands, which she was told to use freely in case she should see anybody or anything approaching from the enemy. The officer, of course, regarded her as an irresponsible negro, and after giving her the assignment took her by the coat collar and gave her a vigorous shake.

"Now, you black rascal," he cried, "if I catch you sleeping at your post I'll shoot you like a dog."

It was a startling position for a stranger in a strange land, especially when that one happened to be a female spy in disguise. The night was very dark and it was beginning to rain. She was all alone now and she could not guess when she would be relieved or just what the next hour might bring forth. Her one thought was to escape. After ascertaining as well as possible the position of the picket on each side of her – each of whom was enjoying the shelter of the nearest tree – she deliberately and noiselessly stepped into the darkness and was soon gliding swiftly through the forest toward the Union lines. She had to make her approach very carefully for she was in as much danger of being shot by her friends as by the enemy, so she spent the remainder of the night within hailing distance of the Union lines, and with the first dawn of morning hoisted the well known signal and was heartily welcomed back to her own camp.

She made her way to the tent containing the hospital nurses and removed as much of the color from her face as was possible with the aid of soap and water. She then made out a report and carried it to the headquarters of General McClellan. He was intensely interested in the news that had been brought him and heartily congratulated the spy on her work. The rifle which she had carried from the Confederate lines was an object of much curiosity, and it is now said to be in one of the museums in the national capitol as a memento of the war.

It was several weeks before the female spy received her second assignment, and then when it came a new disguise was necessary. The African costume was abandoned and she decided to go into the Confederate lines this time in the capacity of an Irish apple woman, so she procured the dress and outfit that was necessary for this impersonation and also practiced the brogue that might be needed to carry her through the emergency. The bridges were not finished across the Chickahominy when she was ready to cross the river, so she packed up her new disguise in the cake and pie basket and swam across the river mounted on her horse, which was known as Frank. Reaching the other side she dismounted and led him to the edge of the water. Giving him a farewell pat she permitted him to swim back to the other side, where a soldier awaited his return.

It was night, and as she did not know the precise distance to the enemy's picket lines she thought it best to avoid the road and consequently determined to spend the night in the swamp. It required some time to put on her new disguise and to feel at home in the clothes. She whimsically said at the time that she thought the best place for her début as an apple woman was the Chickahominy swamp. She did not propose this time to pass the enemy's lines in the night, but to present herself at the picket line at a seasonable hour and to ask admission as one of the fugitives of that section who was flying at the approach of the Yankees.

In crossing the river she had her basket strapped on her back and did not know that its contents were completely drenched until she was required to use them. Later she discovered with much terror that she was suffering from fever and ague as a result of spending the night in the wet clothing in that malaria infested region. Her mind began to wander and she became delirious. There seemed to be the horrors of a thousand deaths centered around her. She was tortured by fiends of every shape and magnitude, but morning came at last and she was aroused from the nightmare which had paralyzed her senses by the roar of the cannon and the screaming of the shells.

The cannonading ceased in a few hours, but the chills and fever clung to the spy and were her constant companion for two days and two nights. At the end of that time she was certainly an object of pity; with no medicine or food and little strength, she was almost in a state of starvation. Her pies and cakes were spoiled and she had no means of procuring more. It was nine o'clock in the morning of the third day after crossing the river when she started to what she thought was the enemy's lines. She traveled from that time until four o'clock in the afternoon and was then deeper in the swamp than when she started. As it was a dark day in every sense of the word, she had neither sun nor compass to guide her, but at five o'clock the booming of cannon came to her like music, because it was the signal that would guide her out of the wilderness. She turned her face in the direction of the scene of action and soon after emerging from the swamp she saw a small white house in the distance.

The house was deserted with the exception of a sick Confederate soldier who lay on a straw tick on the floor in a helpless condition. He had been ill with typhoid fever and was very weak.

He told her, however, that the family who had occupied the house had left some flour and corn meal but did not have time to cook anything for him. This was good news to the exhausted spy, and she soon kindled a fire and in less than fifteen minutes a large hoe cake was in the process of baking. She found some tea packed away in a small basket and the cake being cooked and the tea made she fed the poor famished man as tenderly as if he had been her brother, and after that she tended to the cravings of her own appetite. But it was quite evident that the man could not recover. He was dying. She did everything in her power to make him comfortable, but it was quite plain that he only had a few hours to live. While she stood by his side he said:

"I have a last request to make. If you ever pass through the Confederate camp between this and Richmond inquire for Major McKee of General Ewell's staff and give him a gold watch which you will find in my pocket. He will know what to do with it, and tell him I died happy and peaceful."

His name was Allen Hall. Taking a ring from his finger he tried to put it on hers, but his strength failed and after a pause he said:

"Keep that ring in memory of one whose sufferings you have alleviated and whose soul has been refreshed by your presence in the hour of dissolution."

He folded his hands together as a little child would do at its mother's knee. She gave him some water, raised the window and used her hat for a fan and then sat down, as she put it, "And watched the last glimmering spark of life go out from those beautiful windows of the soul."

He died at twelve o'clock that night and after the involuntary nurse had wrapped the form of her late patient in his winding sheet she laid down in a corner of the room and slept soundly until six o'clock in the morning. It was a curious situation, but it did not seem to affect the nerve of this remarkable woman. She cut a lock of hair from the head of the dead man, took the watch and a small package of letters from his pocket and left the house.

On examining the basket in which she had found the tea she discovered a number of articles which assisted her in assuming a more perfect disguise. There was mustard, pepper, an old pair of green spectacles and a bottle of red ink. Of the mustard she made a strong plaster about the size of a silver dollar and tied it on one side of her face until it blistered thoroughly.

She then removed the blister and put on a large patch of black court plaster. After giving her pale complexion a deep tinge with some ochre which she found in a closet, she put on her green glasses and Irish hat. She had previously made a tour of the house to find the fixings which an Irish woman would be supposed to carry with her in such an emergency, for she fully expected to be searched before she was admitted through the lines.

She followed the Richmond road about five miles before meeting any one. At length she saw a sentinel in the distance, but before he observed her she sat down to rest and prepare her mind for the coming interview. While thus waiting to have her courage reinforced, she took from her basket the black pepper and sprinkled a little of it on her pocket handkerchief, and then applied the moisture to her eyes. The effect of it was all that could be desired, for taking a view of her face in a small mirror which she always carried, she perceived that her eyes had a fine tender expression which added very much to their beauty. She now resumed her journey and displayed a flag of truce, a window curtain which she had brought from the house where she had stopped over night. As she came nearer, the sentinel signaled for her to advance, which she did as fast as she could under the circumstances. He cross questioned her at some length and then permitted her to pass along the road, saying that she might go wherever she pleased.

After thanking the man for his kindness, she went her way toward the Confederate camp. She had not gone far when he called her back and advised her not to stay in the camp over night, adding:

"One of our spies has just come in and reported that the Yankees have finished the bridges across the Chickahominy and intend to attack us either to-day or to-night, but Jackson and Lee are ready for them. We have masked batteries in all parts of the road. There is one over there that'll give them fits, if they come this way."

This was important information, and Miss Edmonds made up her mind at once that she must get all the news that was possible before night and then make her way back to the Union camp before the battle began. At five o'clock that afternoon she met Major McKee, and, carrying out the promise she made to the dying Confederate, she delivered to him the watch and package. She did not require any black pepper to assist the tears in performing their duty, for the sad mementoes which she had just delivered were a forcible reminder of the scenes of the past night, and she could not refrain from weeping. The major, grave and stem as he was, sat there with his face between his hands and sobbed like a child. Soon he rose to his feet, surveyed her from head to foot and said:

"You are a faithful woman and you shall be rewarded."

At his request she consented to show a detachment of the guards the house where Allen's body lay. They made their way there cautiously, lest they should be surprised by the Federals. Miss Edmonds rode at the head of the little band of Confederates as a guide, not knowing but that she was leading them into the jaws of death. They traveled thus for five miles, silently, thoughtfully and stealthily. The sun had gone down when they came in sight of the little white cottage in the forest where she had so recently spent such a strange night. As they drew near and saw no sign of approaching Federals, they regretted that they had not brought an ambulance, but Miss Edmonds did not regret it for the arrangement suited her admirably. They were soon at the gate of the house. The sergeant ordered the corporal to proceed inside with a squad of men and bring out the corpse while he stationed the remaining men to guard all the approaches to the house. He then asked Miss Edmonds to ride down the road a little way to watch out for the Yankees with instructions to ride back as fast as possible if she detected any of the hated tribe.

She assented joyfully. It was the very thing for which she had been watching and waiting. She turned and rode slowly down the road, but not seeing or hearing anything of the Yankees whimsically thought it best to keep on in that direction until she did. She says that she was like the Zouave after the battle of Bull Run who said he was ordered to retreat but not being ordered to halt in any particular place preferred to keep on until he reached New York. So Miss Edmonds preferred to keep on until she reached the Chickahominy where she reported all the information she had gathered to the Federal general who was in charge.

The news that she brought was of the highest importance and proved to be of great assistance to the officers in arranging their final plans for the forth-coming battle. This was the last feat undertaken by Miss Edmonds, and by a curious chain of circumstances it enabled her to take part in one of the most thrilling battles of the war.

The battle of Hanover Court House is counted among the heroic engagements of that year, and was a very important victory for the army of the Potomac.

Three days after this battle while the army was divided by the Chickahominy River, a portion of the troops having crossed over the day before, a most fearful storm swept over the peninsula accompanied by terrible exhibitions of lightning and explosions of thunder. The water came down in torrents and there were great floods, completely engulfing the valley through which the Chickahominy flows and turning the narrow stream into a broad river as well as converting the swamps into lakes.

On the 30th of May, the enemy, taking advantage of this terrible state of affairs, came rushing down upon the Union troops in immense force. A battle opened at about one o'clock in the afternoon and after three hours of desperate fighting General Casey's division, occupying the first line, was compelled to fall back in considerable disorder upon the second line, causing temporary confusion; but the rapid advance of General Heinselman and General Kearney with their divisions soon checked the Confederates.

The enemy, led by Hill and Longstreet, advanced in great columns with three full lines, and came boldly on like an overwhelming wave, as if determined to crush all opposition by the suddenness and fierceness of the attack. It looked as if the Union troops would be annihilated; indeed, it seemed as if the fragments of the army would be driven into the Chickahominy before it would be possible for reinforcements to arrive. It was at this most dramatic stage of the battle that Miss Edmonds became a voluntary orderly to one of the generals. She has told the story in her own words, which cannot be improved upon. It furnishes a fine climax to her sensational career in the army.

"At this time," she says, "I was in military uniform mounted on my horse and acting as orderly for General Kearney. Several times orderlies had been sent with messages and dispatches but no reinforcements had yet arrived, and taking a Federal view of the picture it presented a gloomy appearance. The General reined in his horse abruptly and taking from his pocket an envelope he hastily wrote on the back of it with pencil, 'In the name of God, bring your command to our relief if you have to swim in order to get here – or we are lost.' Handing it to me he said:

"'Go just as fast as that horse can carry you to General G, present this with my compliments and return and report to me.'

"I put poor little 'Reb' over the road at the very top of his speed until he was nearly white with foam, then plunged him into the Chickahominy and swam across the river. I met one general about one hundred rods from the river, making the best of his way towards the bridge. Engineers were at once set to work strengthening the crazy structure, which was swaying to and fro with the rush of the tide. The eager, excited troops dashed into the water waist deep, and getting upon the floating planks went pouring over in massive columns. I preferred to swim my horse back again rather than risk myself upon such a bridge, for I looked every moment to see it give way and engulf the whole division in the turbid waters of the swollen creek. However, all reached the other side in safety and started along the flooded road on the double quick. This was cheering news to carry back to the General, so I started again through the field in order to claim the reward of 'Him who bringeth good tidings.'

"I found the General in the thickest of the fight, encouraging his men and shouting his orders distinctly above the roar and din of battle. Riding up to him and touching my hat I reported:

"'Just returned, sir. General G with his command will be here immediately.'

"It was too good to keep to himself, so he turned to his men and shouted at the top of his voice:

"'Reinforcements! Reinforcements!'

"Then, swinging his hat in the air, he perfectly electrified the whole line as far as his voice could reach and the glorious word 'Reinforcements,' was passed along until that almost exhausted line was re-animated and inspired with new hopes, which led it to ultimate victory."

8

The amazing adventure of Brigadier-General Lafayette C. Baker

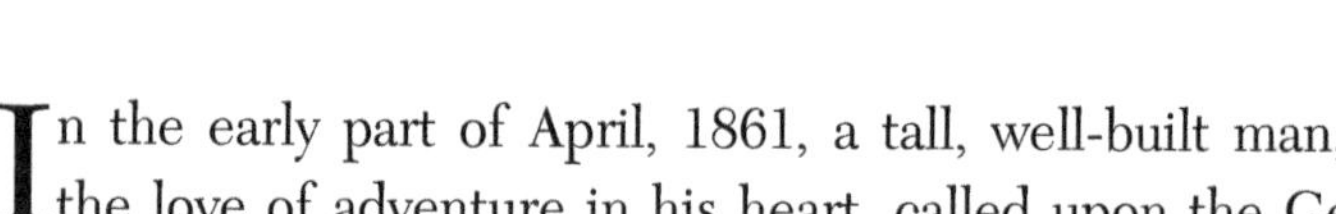

In the early part of April, 1861, a tall, well-built man, with the love of adventure in his heart, called upon the General commanding the Union forces and offered to penetrate the Confederate lines for the purpose of discovering the military secrets of the Southern army.

The volunteer was Lafayette C. Baker, who was to play a most conspicuous part in the Civil War, and the soldier to whom he made his proposal was General Winfield Scott, one of the most distinguished military men in the United States. The interview was epoch-making in its character, and out of it came one of the most amazing adventures in the history of the war.

BRIGADIER-GENERAL LAFAYETTE C. BAKER

Washington was filled with all sorts of men on all sorts of missions at that time, and Scott was not disposed to see the young man from the West. The General, with others in power, had his fill of theorists who offered endless suggestions for the conduct of the war, most of which, when tried, proved to be impracticable. But Baker was the sort of an enthusiast who was not to be daunted. He had journeyed to the National Capital for the purpose of seeing the General and he did not propose to quit until he had accomplished his object. It happened that he was acquainted with Congressman William D. Kelley, a notable member of the House from Philadelphia, and Mr. Kelley, in the kindness of his heart, managed to arrange an interview with General Scott.

The enthusiasm of the man who was willing to risk his life in the cause attracted the attention of the veteran of the Army. Scott had the enviable distinction of having participated in three wars. He rendered distinguished service in the war of 1812, and he was one of the heroes of the Mexican War. Now, as the ranking head of the Army, he was charged with the direction of the Federal forces in the Civil War, although age and increasing infirmities eventually caused him to be shelved in favor of younger men. But in the meantime he was deeply interested in knowing the plans of the Confederates, and he was impressed with the earnestness of Baker.

"You look as if you had the grit and the intelligence for the job," he said, "and I'm going to give you a chance to see what you can do. If you succeed you will be recognized by the Government in a suitable manner."

Baker drew himself up to his full height and there was a flash of fire in his gray eyes as he exclaimed:

"All I ask is this chance – I'll guarantee to make good!"

The General smiled and placed his hand upon the shoulder of the volunteer.

"That's the sort of spirit that wins. Good-by and good luck to you!"

But before Baker left, Scott had pressed ten twenty-dollar gold pieces into his hands.

"You may need it for expenses," he said with a humorous twinkle in his eyes.

Lafayette Baker now possessed the status of an "unofficial spy." He was not commissioned and he was unarmed, but he was satisfied that if he were able to carry out his promise he would not fail to receive governmental recognition. His first move was to contrive some plan that would make his appearance in the camp seem reasonable. He discarded the notion of a disguise as unnecessary and dangerous. He finally hit upon the expedient of pretending to be an itinerant photographer. At that stage of the Civil War picture taking was all the rage and the officers delighted in having themselves photographed in front of their tents, surrounded by their aides.

Baker went to one of the second hand shops in Washington and succeeded in purchasing a camera and a tripod. The fact that the camera was worn out and unworkable did not disturb him in the least. The dealer chuckled at the thought of finding a customer who was willing to pay real money for such junk, little thinking that the paraphernalia was precisely suited to the needs of the purchaser.

All of his preparations were completed on the 11th of July, 1861, and on the morning of that day he began his journey, exclaiming as he did so,

"On to Richmond!"

Baker had been given detailed instructions by General Scott and was told to keep his eyes and ears open during the progress of his trip to the Confederate capital. He had been told to learn the locality, strength and character of the Southern troops and to let no opportunity pass for gaining information of the enemy's fortifications. General Scott was especially anxious to get some definite news concerning the famous Black Horse Cavalry, which had become the bane of the Union Commanders.

Baker began his journey in high spirits. The nature of his services, of course, was not known to the Federal troops and as a consequence he was regarded by them with quite as much interest and curiosity as if he had been within the lines of the enemy.

The Federal Army lay before Washington, guarding the frontier, which stretched from a point three miles below Alexandria toward the Potomac. General Heintzelman was the Provost Marshal and was stationed at this point. Passes were not recognized either by the Union or Confederate armies, and Baker knew that he ran the risk of being arrested as a spy either by the Federal or the Confederate sentinels. However, he knew the attempt to get through both these lines was a part of his self-imposed task. When he was four miles out of the city he reached the headquarters of the Second Maine Regiment. His photographic outfit was slung across his back and the

Colonel of the regiment invited him to take a view of the camp, including his own tent with the principal officers standing in the foreground. As Baker's apparatus was next to worthless, he knew that it would be folly for him to pretend to take the picture, but he was equal to the occasion. After dining with the Colonel, he suggested that he would like to go to a neighboring hill and take views of the encampment and then return to photograph the headquarters. He was soon in the woods, and eluding the guards pushed forward through the tangled undergrowth in the direction of Richmond. After a while he felt that he had crossed the Federal lines, but at that critical moment he was startled by a loud command:

"Who goes there!"

Baker looked up and saw a sentinel standing with lifted gun upon a knoll just beyond the roadside. There was no opportunity for explanation. The guard marched the volunteer in the direction of the Colonel's headquarters. That officer was sure he had caught a spy and escorted by ten men, Baker was sent back along the railroad, the very way he had started, to General Heintzelman's headquarters. He was presented to the General in language that was more expressive than flattering:

"Here's a dirty spy, General – we found him lurking about our camp and trying to get through the lines."

"You contemptible villain!" exclaimed Heintzelman with an oath, "I've got a notion to stand you against the wall and shoot you through the heart."

Baker, with all his courage, quailed before this fiery denunciation. He was in a predicament. His employment by

General Scott was confidential and it might spoil his plan of campaign if he should disclose his identity, but while he was wondering what he should do under the circumstances, General Heintzelman burst forth with another tirade:

"I'll fix you, you rascal!" he exclaimed. "I'll send you to General Scott and I'll wager that he'll teach you a lesson that will last you for the balance of your life."

The captive smiled at this announcement. It fitted in with his own desires so well that he could scarcely conceal his own satisfaction. A guard was placed around him and he was hurried to Washington and into the presence of General Scott. The veteran lifted his eyebrows with surprise and amusement and dismissed the escort.

"Leave this man with me," he said, trying to conceal his smile; "I'll know how to deal with him."

When they were alone the General patted his messenger on the shoulder and said cheerfully:

"This is a complication that I had not anticipated. What are you going to do about it?"

"I'm going to try again," was the prompt reply of Baker, and ten minutes later he was started on his mission for the second time.

Soldiers were arriving in Washington at all hours of the day and night and in an almost unbroken line were marching over a long bridge into Virginia. That night Baker took his position at the end of the bridge and when a regiment came down in considerable disorder he quietly slipped into the ranks, hoping to be borne along with the troops. Unfortunately a lieutenant saw the movement and taking the interloper by the collar put him under guard and sent him back to the rear. He was released with a warning not to repeat the trick.

Another night was spent in Washington, but it was not wholly devoted to sleep. The active mind of the volunteer was busy with new plans and when daylight came he said to himself with the air of a child who is reciting a lesson:

"On to Richmond!"

Before breakfast that morning he had renewed his journey on foot, going through the lower counties of Maryland, toward Fort Tobacco. He traveled thirty-five miles that day and when night came he was so exhausted that he slept like a log. In the morning he gave a negro one of his precious twenty-dollar gold pieces to row him across the river and before noon that day he found himself well within the Confederate lines. The country was wooded and an unfrequented road, whose general direction was toward Richmond, suggested his line of advance into the old dominion. It was a hot day and he was forced to pause frequently to slake his thirst at brooks by the roadside. He had no settled plan of future movements, but trusted to circumstances to steer his course. He was about four miles from the banks of the Potomac when two Confederate soldiers made their appearance and demanded him to give an account of himself. He did so, but his story was evidently discounted, for the soldiers promptly placed him under arrest as a spy. They were friendly guards, however, and accepted an invitation from their prisoner to indulge in a glass of ale at a beer shop in one of the townships through which they passed. One glass, as frequently happens, led to another, until finally the two soldiers fell asleep on the step of the beer house and their prisoner went on his way unmolested.

He proceeded along the road toward Manassas Junction, congratulating himself on his easy escape when four cavalrymen suddenly came out of the brush and ordered him to halt. They drew their sabers and commanded him to surrender. He pretended surprise.

"I'm a law abiding citizen," he exclaimed, "unarmed and on my way to Richmond, where I have business."

One of the men dismounted and proceeded to search him and succeeded in finding a number of letters. It was just the thing that Baker wanted, for two of these missives were notes of introduction to prominent men in Richmond. In spite of this, the four soldiers directed Baker to proceed to Brentsville, about ten miles distant. They rode all the way and kept him on foot between them. Brentsville was reached about ten o'clock that night and the prisoner was immediately taken to the headquarters of General Bonham of South Carolina, who was in command at that vicinity. The General, who was in full dress uniform, took a seat opposite Baker and began to question him.

"Where do you come from and where are you going?" he asked.

"I come from Washington and I am on my way to Richmond."

"What do you mean by coming inside of my lines!" he exclaimed.

Baker's face in the language of the movies "registered" intense surprise.

"I'm a loyal and peaceful citizen of the United States, engaged in an honorable and legitimate pursuit. I have business in Richmond and desire to get there at the earliest possible moment."

The Confederate General laughed mirthlessly.

"Well, I'll see that you get there and in quick order. I believe you're a Union spy and I'm going to send you to General Beauregard."

General Bonham handed a sealed letter to a lieutenant who was standing near by and said:

"Put this man in irons and take him to General Beauregard's headquarters."

So at midnight, expostulating all the way, he was compelled to go on foot in the direction of Manassas Junction. When he protested against being compelled to walk such a distance he was told that he had chosen that mode of conveyance and ought not to find fault with it. The party arrived at Manassas Junction at daylight and went at once to General Beauregard's headquarters, which were located at the Wiere House. The prisoner was completely exhausted from his walk and he lay down in front of the house and went to sleep. He awoke at nine o'clock and found himself in charge of a guard, who told him that General Beauregard had expressed a desire to see him.

General Beauregard sat in front of a desk, surrounded by members of his staff. An open letter lay before him. He pointed to it, frowningly, and said:

"I see that you have been taken inside of our lines. What explanation have you to make?"

Lafayette Baker had been cross-examined so often during his brief career as a military spy that he was becoming used to the ordeal. He had his story by heart and he proceeded to tell it glibly.

"I am from Washington and I am on my way to Richmond where I have private business requiring my attention. I have not intended to violate any law, regulation or military rule of the Confederate Army."

The General turned to a member of his staff and began whispering. The prisoner watched him anxiously. The letters that had been taken from him named him as Samuel Munson and he realized that it would not do to forget the appellation. He had assumed that name because he had learned that several families by the name of Munson belonged in Knoxville, Tennessee, and he had known a son of Judge Munson during the time he lived in California. While this thought was running through his mind the General finished his conversation with his staff officer and once more turned to the spy.

"So you are going to Richmond, are you?"

The prisoner smiled.

"That was my intention," he replied, "but of course you are to be the judge in that matter. If it is your desire, I am willing to return to Washington."

General Beauregard shook his head.

"No," he said, with a slight trace of sarcasm in his voice. "I prefer that you should go to Richmond. Where do you reside?"

"I have lived in California for the last ten years, but formerly lived in the South in Knoxville, Tennessee."

"How long has it been since you were in Knoxville?"

"Ten or twelve years."

"What is your name?"

"Samuel Munson," replied Baker with cheerful mendacity.

General Beauregard looked at the prisoner intently and then suddenly exclaimed:

"Yes, yes, I know that is the name on the letters that were found in your possession, but I'd like to know what your name was before you became a spy."

If he expected to catch his man unaware, he was disappointed for Baker, looking at him with assumed dignity, said:

"I am no spy."

The General arose from his chair and paced up and down the room several times. Presently he halted and pointing out of the window said:

"Do you see that tree?"

"I do."

"Well, I half believe that you are a spy and if I was sure of it I would hang you on that tree as a warning to all other spies."

Baker looked at him reproachfully and not without a secret feeling of fear. The General called to one of his attendants.

"Orderly," he commanded, "take this man out and put him in the guard house."

Five minutes later the adventurer found himself inside of a log house within a stockade. The discreet use of one of his gold pieces secured him a warm breakfast and later in the day he was permitted to go outside in the care of a guard. The two men were soon on good terms and the guard did not disdain the offer of a drink with his prisoner. Before they returned, Baker had the satisfaction of seeing all the troops in the vicinity of Manassas Junction – including the famous Black Horse Cavalry concerning which General Scott was anxious to obtain information.

The volunteer spy now had important information which would be of great value to General Scott, but he had no means of conveying it to the Union Commander. Indeed, he was kept under lock and key with no means to communicate with the outside world. Perhaps his guards repented having given him so much liberty. If so they did not propose to repeat the mistake. During the long watches of the night he had time to think over his position, and to consider his plans for the future. As a result of this he abandoned all thought of trying to escape – at least at that stage of the adventure. His one desire was to reach Richmond, and thus carry out his original design. But if he were kept confined there would not be much prospect of reaching the Confederate capital. Curiously enough, the thought of being shot as a spy did not enter his thoughts at that time. He was so much engrossed in his mission that he did not think of the risk he was running. All during that night his one thought was:

How shall I get to Richmond?

Just before daylight the answer came in the most abrupt and unexpected manner. One of his guards aroused him, shouting:

"Hey there, wake up and get ready for a journey! You've got to go to Richmond and give an account of yourself to Jeff Davis!"

Baker could have cried with joy. The one thing he most desired had come about without any effort on his part. He cheerfully arose and won the good will of the guard by his seeming docility. He was taken to the station and placed on a freight car, along with some others who were also going to Richmond. Evidently he was regarded as an important prisoner, for he was carefully guarded during every stage of the journey. That trip during the night, over a badly constructed road was a nightmare, long to live in the memory of Lafayette Baker. But the prospect of actually setting foot in the Confederate capital kept him in the best of spirits and enabled him to exchange jests with his captors.

On the arrival in Richmond he expected to be taken to Libby Prison, concerning the horrors of which he had heard a great deal from Union soldiers who had been captured in some of the early skirmishes of the war. But instead of that he was conveyed to a room on the third story of an engine house in the city. His apartment was large and airy, and was all that could be desired. He was treated with great consideration, but was guarded with scrupulous care. Evidently the officers felt that they had no ordinary prisoner in their charge. The cause of this extreme courtesy became evident on the morning of the second day after Baker's arrival in Richmond when he was informed that President Davis desired to interview him. The head of the Confederacy had his headquarters in the Spottswood House whence the Northern spy was escorted. Baker expected to find much formality there, but to his surprise found Mr. Davis in his shirt sleeves and without collar and tie. He was evidently very busy because his desk was filled with papers and there were a number of persons waiting to have a talk with him. He motioned

Baker to a seat without looking at him, and continued with some writing with which he was engaged when the prisoner was brought into his room. Presently he turned to the suspect and said abruptly:

"They say your name is Samuel Munson?"

"Yes, sir," replied the cheerful fabricator, "that is my name."

"I understand," said the civil chief of the seceding States, toying with his pen, "that you have been in Washington recently. What can you tell me about conditions there?"

"Not much," was the answer, "except that there is a great deal of excitement and confusion there."

"How many troops do you think there are in Washington and vicinity at the present time?"

"That is a pretty difficult question to answer, but there are probably from 75,000 to 100,000, with more arriving all the while."

Mr. Davis seemed to ponder over this for some time, and then looking his caller in the eye, he said,

"I presume that you know you are suspected of being a spy?"

The look of injured innocence which appeared upon the face of Lafayette Baker would have done credit to a professional actor. Nevertheless he evaded a direct answer by saying:

"No man is safe from accusation in times like the present."

"But what have you to say for yourself?"

"Nothing except that I defy my accusers to prove their charges."

"It seems to me," said Mr. Davis, "that some one said you were a Southern man."

"Yes, sir, I came originally from Knoxville. The members of my family lived there for years, but in recent times I have lived in California."

"Have you any way of proving that?"

The alleged Mr. Munson shrugged his shoulders.

"I am afraid I cannot find anyone here to identify me."

The President of the Confederacy smiled a somewhat sarcastic smile.

"Perhaps we may be able to help you out in that respect. There is a Knoxville man in the city and as soon as I am able to locate him I will have you meet him."

This was startling news indeed and it came near shaking the self-assurance of the volunteer spy. But before he had time to make any reply he found himself being escorted out of the room and taken to his place of confinement in the engine house. He was treated as kindly as before, but he realized that the watch upon him was closer than ever. He did some serious thinking that night. As he looked out of the barred windows and up into the unpitying stars he felt that he had reached a real crisis in his life.

One of two things would happen. Either he would escape from his place of confinement, and attempt to reach the North, or he would be shot as a spy. All of the chances seemed to point to his execution on the charge of spying.

But his naturally buoyant disposition came to his aid, and when morning arrived he was taking a more cheerful view of the future. That day he was taken before President Davis and submitted to a further cross-examination. The Chief of the Confederacy appeared to be more anxious to get reliable information concerning the Union forces than to prove that Baker was a spy.

"Who is in command of the Yankees at this time?" he asked.

"General Scott," was the truthful reply.

"Where is he?"

"In Washington."

"Ah, then he is not in charge of the troops?"

"No, sir, I believe that General McDowell is in active command of the forces in the field."

This was correct, and Baker in making the statement felt that he was not giving away any of the secrets of the war. But the information interested the President and he turned aside and talked with several of his advisers who were in the room. In the meanwhile he made a gesture to indicate that he was through with Mr. Baker, alias Mr. Munson, and the spy was led from the room and once again taken to his prison in the engine house. In spite of his optimistic nature these repeated cross-examinations were beginning to unnerve him. He was afraid that he might be tripped up in some of his answers, and then he felt sure that he would be stood up against a wall and shot. He felt that such a procedure would make him a martyr, but he had a very natural desire to postpone his martyrdom as long as possible.

His real ordeal was to come on the following day. Shortly after breakfast he learned that Mr. Davis desired to see him again. And he learned something else that caused him much perturbation. It was that a Knoxville man had been located in Richmond and that he had been sent for to identify the supposed Mr. Munson. Baker tried hard to screw up his courage for the interview. He was at a loss as to how he should act and talk. It was certain that the man did not know him and in such an event he would be in the position of being condemned as an impostor and a spy. While he was preparing to go over to the Spottswood House he heard one of his captors speak of a Mr. Brock of Knoxville, who had also been summoned to meet the President. Baker grasped at this as a drowning man grabs at a straw. All the way to the hotel he racked his brain in the effort to work out a plan of action. But he could reach no definite conclusion. He would have to be guided entirely by circumstances. One thing he did do was to refresh his mind as to certain names and places in Knoxville. When he reached the headquarters of the Confederate Government he found Mr. Davis talking with a man in a frock coat and a slouch hat. At first he supposed that this must be Brock, but fortunately he learned that it was Robert Toombs, and was thereby saved from making a break that might have caused his undoing. In a moment the President turned to the spy.

"Hello, Munson," he said, "I have sent for a man who has lived in Knoxville for many years, and he will be able to tell us if you are the person you claim to be. Take a seat. He'll be here in a few minutes."

Baker sat on a chair facing the door and anxiously waited for the man who was to give the verdict. The moments went by on leaden heels. He could feel the cold sweat coming out on his brow. But he had courage and he was resourceful. Once the door opened and a messenger came in. Baker half rose to his feet, but caught himself in time. He could not afford to make a mistake. The President and Toombs talked together as if oblivious to his presence. Presently Toombs threw himself on a couch in a corner of the room and Mr. Davis busied himself with some papers on his desk. The spy kept his eyes glued upon the door. Out of it would walk his doom or his deliverance – he could not tell which. Suddenly when the strain was beginning to seem too great for further endurance, the door was opened and a middle-aged man entered the room. He hesitated for a moment and looked about him inquiringly. Baker felt that he must be the man. He did not hesitate for the fraction of a moment, but jumping up and hurrying toward the newcomer he held out his hand and exclaimed in a tone of great cordiality:

"Why, hello, Brock, how are you, anyhow?"

The surprised visitor did not have time to think. He accepted the proffered hand in a mechanical manner and said slowly:

"You – you are – "

"Sam Munson, of course. Don't you remember me?"

"Judge Munson's son?"

"Certainly – but it's been ten years since we've met. I'm surely glad to see you. How are you, anyhow?"

"I'm right well," said the stampeded one, "and how are you?"

"Well, I haven't been very well, but the sight of you is a cure for sore eyes. They've locked me up on suspicion, and you've just come in the nick of time. They wanted someone to let them know that I was really Sam Munson. How long has it been since you've been in the old town?"

"Two years," said Brock, watching the other man intently.

"Well, it's been ten since I was there, and I'll bet they've had some big changes in that time."

"Rather!"

"By the way," continued Baker, trying to prevent the other from having time to think, "you remember the Bradleys, don't you? Well, I heard not long ago that Sue Bradley had married – married some fellow from Chattanooga. She was a mighty fine girl was Sue, and the fellow that got her got a prize."

Well, to make a long story short the bluff worked – not like a charm, but with sufficient smoothness to enable the nervy spy to save his life. Brock and Baker had one or two more interviews, and by ransacking his brain for incidents he had learned about the prominent people of Knoxville he finally persuaded Brock that he was really Sam Munson. The visitor even went so far as to apologize for his seeming inability to place his fellow townsman at first sight.

"But you must remember that it has been many years since you left the old town, Sam. You've changed a lot since then."

"Don't mention it," was the hearty response. "I'd have been the same if I had been in your place. But you've done me a good turn, and I won't forget it."

There was no doubt of the good turn – if saving a man from being shot as a spy can be placed in that category.

As a result of the business Baker was not released, but he was placed under parole. This gave him the right to wander about Richmond at will – the very privilege he most desired. If he had planned the thing in advance it could not have worked out more to his liking. He was free to go and come as he pleased, and he was actually under the patronage and the protection of the Confederate Government!

For two days and two nights he roamed about until he became as familiar with conditions in Richmond as if he were a resident. He obtained a mass of data concerning military plans and proposed movements, learned where troops were quartered and where fortifications were being erected. Most of this information he carried in his head, but in a few instances he made notes of a character which were intelligible to himself, but which were not likely to be decipherable to any one else. Finally the time came when he knew more than "was good" for himself, from a Confederate point of view. The question was how to get this knowledge to the Federal Government. The fact that he had been before Mr. Davis and was now at liberty made him seem harmless to most of the officers in Richmond. He became personally acquainted with some of them. One was the Provost Marshal, and so, one day, when he asked that official for a pass to permit him to visit Fredericksburg it was granted without any hesitation.

He proceeded to that place without any difficulty. Once or twice he was halted by sentinels, but the production of his pass was all that was needed to permit him to go on his way. On the night of the day he reached Fredericksburg he parted with another of his precious gold pieces to a negro who rowed him across the Rappahannock. He drew a breath of relief when he reached the other side of the stream, and yet he realized that his dangers had only begun. That night he slept in a haystack – slept the sleep of a dog-tired man, if not of the just. When he awoke at dawn he discovered signs of activity in the vicinity of the barn where he had slept and he knew that he was being pursued. He lay very quiet and listened. Voices were shouting and it did not take him long to learn that a squad of Confederate cavalry was on the hunt and that a number of horsemen surrounded the barn.

He shuddered at the thought of the consequences. He had plenty of courage but he did not relish the thought of being caught like a rat in a trap. He had provided himself with a revolver, and he firmly resolved that if he were detected he would not give his life easily. He grasped the weapon, and lay very, very quiet. He was almost afraid to breathe. Presently one of the cavalrymen dismounted and flourishing his sword began a search of the barn. Some of those on the outside were shouting instructions to the searcher, and he responded cheerily. He poked his sword here and there in the hay rick, calling meanwhile on any supposed fugitive to surrender if he did not want to be killed. At one time the point of the sword just grazed Baker's boots. He could have screamed with nervousness, but by a super-human effort he managed to keep perfectly quiet. And by so doing he saved his life, for the officer turning to his companions called:

"He ain't here, boys – we might as well move on!"

They rode off, to the great joy of the hidden man. He remained still until the sound of the horses' hoofs had died out in the distance, and then he crept from his place of concealment more dead than alive. He waited for a long while and then crept out of the barn and made for the woods. How long he struggled through the woods he could not tell, but he was so hungry, and faint and footsore that nothing seemed to make any difference. That night he managed to get supper in a hut owned by a poor colored man, and afterwards tried to find just where the Potomac was located. When he reached that stream he discovered an old row boat. The owner of it was lying, half asleep, on the banks of the river. Baker invited him to sell the boat, offering the last of his gold pieces for craft, but the owner indignantly refused saying that he would not part with it for any price.

This was discouraging, and in lieu of anything better to do he lay down and went to sleep, with the hard earth for a couch, and the shining stars for his covering. He awakened just before daylight with every bone in his body aching, and an intense yearning for home. The owner of the boat was still asleep, and his craft lay anchored in the water. It did not take Baker long to come to a decision. At that stage of his career larceny seemed a very petty offense. He crept down to the water side and climbing into the boat began to row gently into the stream. The job was not an easy one because the oars were broken and decayed. However, by great care he managed to get the boat into the middle of the stream. At that moment the owner awoke, and when he discovered what had happened sent up a series of ear-splitting screams.

"Come back with that boat, you thief," he yelled, "or I'll kill you."

Baker did not fear anything from the man, but in a few moments he saw that three or four soldiers had suddenly appeared upon the scene, and were talking with the distracted owner of the boat. They grasped the situation at a glance, and ordered him to halt at the risk of his life. Instead of halting he pulled harder than ever. Without another word one of the soldiers raised his gun and fired. The shot struck one of the oars and shattered it. Once again came the command to halt and once again the fleeing man renewed his efforts as best he could with the broken oar. This time three of the soldiers aimed at the man in the boat. There was a hissing sound, Baker ducked and the bullets went skimming across the water. The situation was becoming perilous. The fugitive plied his one good oar, and worked the stump of the other with great vigor, and in this way managed to lengthen the distance between himself and the shore. A final volley came from the soldiers and this time the shots fell short of the mark by several yards.

Baker breathed freely for the first time since he had boarded the boat. He was out of danger for the time being. All depended now upon his ability to get to the Maryland side of the stream. It was a hard job, but he stuck at it with the persistence of a desperate man, and eventually felt the small craft grazing the beach. He felt a strong desire to cheer, but he overestimated his strength, for the moment he climbed out of the boat he fell to the ground, exhausted. The perils and the privations he had undergone were enough to kill a less resolute and less hardy man. He lay on the shore for more than an hour, until finally a farmer passing that way halted and picked him up. He was taken to a farmhouse, and given a meal which he ate with the ravenousness of a wolf. His hosts were naturally filled with curiosity, but he felt that discretion was the part of wisdom and he declined to reveal his identity, or the cause of the plight in which he had been found.

That night, in spite of the protests of the farmer, he resumed his journey to Washington. He walked the greater part of the night and slept in a barn as usual. He begged his breakfast and then started on his last lap to the National Capital. It was some time before he felt that he was out of danger, but finally the dome of the Capitol came into view, and he knew then that he was safe and that his remarkable adventure was to be a success. It was nearly noon, and there was a broiling sun when he finally reached the streets of Washington. He did not wait to eat or to make himself presentable, but headed immediately for the headquarters of General Scott. The attendant at the door repulsed him and said that it would be impossible to see the General at that time. Baker knew that this reception was caused by his disreputable appearance, and once he was sure that Scott was in his room, he pushed the man aside and bolted into the apartment where the head of the army was making his headquarters. The General was seated at a desk and as the strange looking specimen of humanity stood beside him, he said rather gruffly:

"Well, sir, what can I do for you?"

Baker threw out his arms in a gesture of entreaty and said with a wan smile:

"Why, General, don't you know me?"

The veteran rose to his feet and closely scrutinized the speaker, and then he said, with a welcoming smile and outstretched hand:

"Well, by all that's holy, it's Baker!"

He would not let him tell his story then, but insisted upon his taking a hearty dinner and making himself comfortable. After that the adventurous one sat down and gave a detailed account of his exploits from the time he left Washington. He presented a complete report of all he had learned while in Richmond, and furnished him with data concerning the size and movements of the Confederate soldiers. Other members of the staff were called into consultation, and after their talk had been concluded Baker was plied with questions which he had no difficulty in answering. It was dusk before he had talked himself out, and then the General took him by the hand and thanked him for what he had done for the Government.

"You have more than made good," he said, "and I will see that you get the recognition which you deserve."

On the following morning General Scott walked over to the War Department, and when he returned he carried with him a commission which made Lafayette Baker an agent in the secret service of the War Department. From that time until the close of the war he participated actively in the work of both the War and State Departments. He was recognized by President Lincoln and became intimately associated with Secretary Stanton. As the result of all this he was made Provost General and later was promoted to the post of Brigadier-General in the army.

9

The mysterious "F" and the captured troopers

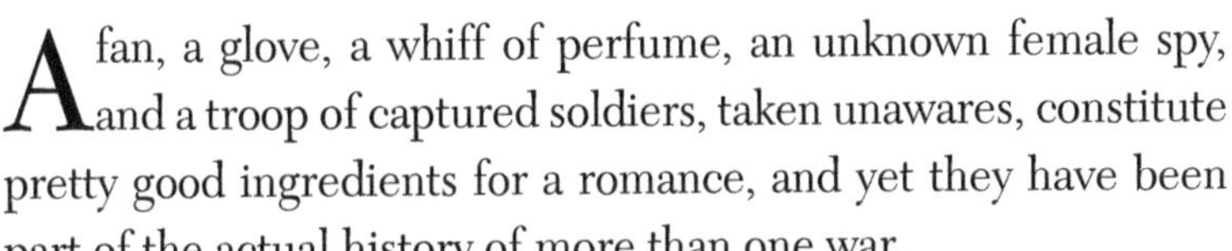

A fan, a glove, a whiff of perfume, an unknown female spy, and a troop of captured soldiers, taken unawares, constitute pretty good ingredients for a romance, and yet they have been part of the actual history of more than one war.

During the Civil War the Union troops occupied the territory known as Fairfax Court House for a considerable period. It was in Virginia, and might fairly be said to be "the enemy's country." It was one of those army outposts where the men are called upon to do a great deal of watchful waiting. The Union soldiers and the residents of the community came to know one another pretty well, and in the course of time there came that familiarity which breeds contempt of danger. There were social affairs and the people came and went as they pleased.

General Stoughton was in charge of the small Union force which was in control of the town, and there is nothing in the official reports to indicate that he was remiss in any way. But some of the men began to feel that everything was not as it should be. It was rumored that at least one of the women in the place was supplying information to the enemy. Just who it was could not be determined, but presently the word went around that the mysterious spy was known only by the letter "F."

Mosby's raiders were performing sensational feats in many parts of Virginia at that time, and it was hinted that they were in the vicinity of Fairfax Court House. One day one of the charming Southern girls of the town went out horseback riding with one of the Union officers. It was a delightful trip and the soldier greatly enjoyed the conversation of his companion, who was a cultivated woman, who, while naturally having much love for her own people, insisted that she had no feeling against the "Yankees." During the return home she became separated from him, and when he rejoined her, found that she was talking to a man by the roadside, in civilian attire. Not much was thought of the incident at the time, but later it was reported that the stranger was not only connected with the Confederate Army, but was actually on the staff of the famous Mosby.

The house occupied by General Stoughton at Fairfax Court House was one of those Southern mansions which are so familiar in Virginia. It was of brick, with a porch, and covered with creeping vines which gave it a most picturesque appearance. The halls were wide and the rooms large and airy. It is not hard to imagine that the ample drawing-room must have been the scene of many festivities in ante-bellum days. In a word, it was just the sort of setting that was necessary for the remarkable adventure in which a girl, a famous scout and a captured general were to be the central figures.

One day a young Union officer entered the drawing-room of this house, and looking about him discovered a fan and a pair of gloves upon the large center table. There was the scent of a faint perfume in the apartment and following it he came across a beautiful girl to whom the articles belonged. He returned them with a gallantry which it might be supposed was foreign to a Northerner, but which as a matter of fact was quite as common as it was in those living south of Mason and Dixon's line. He was fascinated with the girl and she betrayed just enough interest in him to make him want to dance attendance upon her. His duties were not particularly trying at that time and as a consequence he managed to spend a great deal of his time in her company.

Her name – well, he heard it, but it did not make much of an impression upon his mind. It is enough to say that from that time the war seemed to be of secondary importance compared to the ardent affection he felt for the young woman. They walked together and they talked together and he lived in a Paradise of his own making, none the less attractive because it happened to be a Fool's Paradise. Even after the incident which caused such a stir at the time, he defended her from the charge of deceit, so far as he was concerned. But it is very evident that information concerning the conditions about the outpost began to filter into the Confederate lines. Through some mysterious agency all of the details concerning the topography of the camp found its way to General Stuart, the Confederate cavalry leader, and then one evening the thing happened which caused consternation in the North, and was received with joy and laughter in the South.

Mosby, the Confederate Guerrilla, from time to time, obtained information concerning the outpost at Fairfax Court House, and he finally determined to raid it in the hope of making some sensational captures. His little band, which had been recruited from Stuart's Cavalry, was eager for the venture, and held themselves in readiness for the order from their chief. Mosby, who had the loyalty of his men in an intense degree, was one of the remarkable men of the Civil War. He weighed only one hundred and twenty-five pounds and was about five feet, eight inches in height. His face was clean cut and smooth shaven and he had straight, firm lips and a nose that has been described as resembling an eagle's beak. He was just the type of man who might be expected to engage in dangerous adventure without the thought of the consequences.

The affair took place on the eighth of March, 1863. Mosby had been with his Rangers only a month, but already he was gaining a name for himself in all parts of the country. Fairfax Court House at this time was surrounded by large numbers of Union soldiers. Centreville, only a few miles away, contained a brigade of trained men. Still another brigade of mixed troops was located on the pike, near the town. This would seem to be pretty dangerous territory for a small body of raiders, but Mosby had not been receiving information for days without understanding the situation fully. He knew that there was one weak link in the chain of defenses and he knew precisely where to look for it. He proceeded in the direction of this weak spot, followed by twenty-nine of his most daring men. It was pitch dark and impossible to see more than a few feet ahead. Presently they found themselves in the Court House Square, in the center of the town. A picket coming out of the darkness called out:

"Who goes there?"

"A friend," came the reply in a muffled voice.

"Advance and give the countersign," came from the sentinel.

Two of Mosby's men did advance, but they did not give the countersign. On the contrary they threw a coat about the man's head, and before he realized what was going on he had been tied and gagged, and placed near the roadside where he was not likely to do any damage to the expedition. The men were now given specific directions by Mosby as to their duties. The proof that he had been in receipt of confidential messages from the outpost was shown by the fact that he was able to direct each of the men to the particular place where he would find a particular Union officer. They separated and went in squads to different parts of the city. Mosby was particularly anxious to capture Colonel Wyndham, because that officer had sent him a tantalizing message only a few days before; but when he arrived at Wyndham's tent he discovered that his man was not there. As a matter of fact the officer had been summoned to Washington only that morning and thus escaped the humiliation of being captured by Mosby.

In the meanwhile, as his officers went about their various assignments, the chief raider made for the headquarters of General Stoughton. The large front door was unlocked, of course, and Mosby proceeded upstairs to the room which he knew was occupied by the Union officer. He tapped at the door and in a little while it was opened by a young lieutenant who was only partly dressed. He rubbed his eyes and demanded to know the cause of such a visit at such an unearthly hour. Mosby, who seemed to be enjoying the situation, took him to one side and ordered him to take care not to speak loudly or he would shoot him instantly. He demanded to be taken to the bedside of General Stoughton, and as the young man was unarmed, and startled into the bargain, he complied with the request. Once by the bedside the Guerrilla Chieftain gave the sleeping man a terrific whack that awakened him and brought him out of bed in a hurry. He was furious, but before he could say a word the invader said in a tragic whisper:

"Did you ever hear of John S. Mosby?"

"Certainly," was the quick rejoinder. "Have you captured him?"

"No," was the laughing reply, "but he has captured you."

It was humiliating, but General Stoughton was unarmed and perfectly helpless. He was compelled to dress and to go with his captor, who by this time was reinforced by a number of his men. They went in the direction of the Court House Square where they found the remainder of the raiders, with a large number of prisoners lined up and ready for departure. There were in all, fifty or sixty prisoners and fifty-eight horses. In the darkness some of the prisoners escaped. As the party passed a dwelling in the town a voice from an upper window demanded to know who they were. It happened to be the Lieutenant-Colonel of a New York Regiment. Two of Mosby's men were sent into the house to add him to the prizes already in hand but he managed to elude them and to escape.

But how did Mosby and his men get out of Fairfax Court House without arousing the soldiers in the vicinity? Let that be told by Mr. John W. Munson, who was one of the famous raiders, and who has written a most entertaining story of their exploits. "It was always Mosby's care," he says, "to get his men out of the troubles into which he led them. The troops in the town knew of his presence, but each man of them seemed to be looking out for himself, and there was no concert of action. Mosby started toward Fairfax Station to throw his pursuers off their guard, and then suddenly turned toward Centreville. To pass that point meant a great deal to him. The heavy guns looked down frowningly on him only a few hundred yards away, and the Sentinels on the works with 'Who goes there?' hailed him as he passed under them, but he made no reply. Silently the little troop passed along by the big guns of the forts with their prisoners and vanished into the darkness. Captain Barker, one of the prisoners, made a dash toward the fort but was shot at by one of the guerrillas and recaptured just as his horse fell into a ditch.

"One more serious danger confronted Mosby. Cub Run, just beyond Centreville, was overflowing. Back of the little band of raiders was the fort with its brigade of soldiers, soon to be, if not already alarmed; in front of them a raging torrent. There was not an instant of hesitation but, plunging into the mad stream, the whole party swam safely across, although many were carried downstream with the current. Once on the other side pursuit seemed almost impossible and, as the sun rose above the eastern horizon, Mosby breathed his first sigh of relief. Even at that hour he knew that he had graven his name in history never to be effaced. He had performed another feat entirely new in the annals of war, and one that was never to be repeated. In time he reached Culpepper Court House and turned his prisoners over to General Fitz Hugh Lee, who was a classmate of General Stoughton's at West Point."

In the morning Lieutenant-Colonel Johnston started in pursuit of Mosby, but it was too late to capture him or to save the prisoners who had been caught so cleverly. The news spread to all parts of the country and was given an importance far beyond its military meaning. It was humiliating, of course, but it did not have any positive effect upon the remaining days of the war. The most interesting comment, as might be expected, came from President Lincoln, who, when informed that one of his generals and a large number of horses had been captured said, dryly:

"I'm sorry about the horses. I can make Brigadier-Generals easily, but I can't make horses."

But the Confederates were not disposed to look upon the matter so lightly. They knew the value of such an exploit in stirring up the enthusiasm of the people, and Mosby was advertised as a popular hero. General Stuart went so far as to issue a special order proclaiming the incident. It read as follows:

"Captain John S. Mosby has for a long time attracted the attention of his generals by his boldness, skill and success, so signally displayed in his numerous forays upon the invaders of his native State.

None know his daring enterprise and dashing heroism better than these foul invaders though strangers themselves to such noble traits.

His late brilliant exploit, the capture of General Stoughton, U. S. A., two captains, thirty other prisoners, together with their arms, equipments and fifty-eight horses, justifies this recognition in General Orders. The feat, almost unparalleled in the war, was performed in the midst of the enemy's troops, at Fairfax Court House, without loss to Virginia.

The gallant band of Captain Mosby share the glory as they did the danger of this enterprise, and are worthy of such a leader."

Secretary of War Stanton was very angry over the incident. He felt that it was the result of bad management in permitting Union secrets to be discovered by the enemy and he was determined to know just how it had happened. Secretary Stanton sent for General Lafayette C. Baker, then Chief of the Federal Secret Service, and instructed him to make a thorough investigation and to make any arrests that might be deemed necessary. Baker had already made a survey of the grounds at Fairfax Court House, and was familiar with the incidents of the raid. He was perfectly satisfied that the Union soldiers had been betrayed by a spy. And he came to another important conclusion.

It was that the work had been done by a woman spy!

How could he ascertain the identity of the woman and how could he prove her guilt? These were not the sort of questions to be easily answered. Baker suspected the daughter of one of the leading citizens of Fairfax Court House, but he had too much experience in handling delicate matters of the war to think of arresting a woman without having proof of her guilt. It would not do to place the case in the hands of the soldiers. Their methods were likely to be crude, and besides might cause complications. He thought over the matter for some time and then he made a momentous decision. He decided to place the case in the hands of a woman operative in his own office.

It was to be a case of woman against woman!

The woman operative, who shall have to be known as Miss Clarke, prepared for her part with the greatest care. She even perfected herself in the charming Southern dialect so that she should be immediately taken for a daughter of the Sunny South. It was probably a week after the Mosby raid that a fine-looking and apparently embarrassed woman arrived at Fairfax Court House. Finally she managed to enlist the attention of the young woman who was known all through the transaction as "F." The stranger, with feminine impulsiveness, gave her complete confidence to "F." She said that she was greatly attached to the Confederate cause, that she was really a friend and an agent of the South and that she wanted advice and assistance in an effort to reach Warrington. "F," who was the spy that had betrayed Stoughton to Mosby, literally received the newcomer with open arms. She took her to her own home where she was given a warm reception. Miss Clarke was given a repast which included corn muffins, and when they were placed before her she exclaimed:

"This makes me feel that I am home again in the good old South. It has been terrible to have to live in the North with those

Yankees. I have never seen a corn cake since I left the Virginia line."

Everybody laughed at this and everybody was happy. It really seemed like a family reunion. The visitor was petted and patronized and made to feel that she was a person of great importance. And why not? Wasn't she engaged in carrying dispatches to the leaders of the Confederacy – dispatches which might result in the downfall of the Yankee Government? They forebore to ask her the nature of the confidential information which she claimed to be taking to Warrington. Naturally she would be reluctant to impart that even to such good friends as they had shown themselves.

How did Miss Clarke feel under these circumstances? Did she have qualms of conscience at the thought of eating the bread of the family she might soon be called upon to denounce? Not in the least. She knew that the young woman before her had already betrayed the Union soldiers from a sense of loyalty to her section, and Miss Clarke did not have the slightest compunction about betraying "F" in turn. But the thing was to get the proof. She could give evidence that the family of "F" sympathized with the Confederacy and was willing to do anything to aid them, but that was not sufficient for her purpose. How could she get evidence – documentary evidence if possible?

The answer came quicker than she had hoped for. "F" invited her to her bedroom, and when they had closed the door said to the visitor,

"I have something I am going to show you. I think it will interest you for we are engaged in the same cause."

MAJOR-GENERAL J. E. B. STUART

With that she reached under the mattress and brought forth a document which she handed to her visitor. Miss Clarke read it with glowing eyes. It ran as follows:

TO ALL WHOM IT MAY CONCERN, KNOW YE: That reposing special confidence in the patriotism and fidelity of "F," I, James E. B. Stuart, by virtue of the power vested in me as Brigadier-General in the provisional army of the Confederate States of America, do hereby appoint and commission her my honorary aide-de-camp, to rank as such from this date.

She will be obeyed, respected and admired by all lovers of a noble nature.

Given under my hand and seal at the headquarters Cavalry Brigade at Camp Beverly the Seventh day of October, A.D., 1861, and the first year of our independence.

(Signed) J. E. B. STUART,
By the General: L. TIEMAN,
Assistant Adjutant General.

Here was evidence of a most damaging character. Miss Clarke could scarcely restrain her emotions at the important discovery. "F" noticed this and instead of suspecting that all was not well, took the actions of her companion as the natural expressions of feeling under the circumstances. She put a question to the other:

"Don't you feel frightened sometimes – you are engaged in very dangerous work."

"I know that very well," replied Miss Clarke, "but I am sustained by the thought that I am doing it for the sake of my country."

This was followed by an embrace on the part of the two women – both spies, but only one conscious of the true conditions. It might be supposed that having obtained proof of the identity and the complicity of "F" that Miss Clarke might go on her way. But she remained for twenty-four hours longer and in that time obtained a mass of information, not only concerning the suspected woman, but also about the location and the movement of the Southern troops. Finally she departed – departed with another kiss and embrace.

Two days later Sergeant Odell, connected with the staff of General Baker, called at the residence of one of the leading citizens of Fairfax Court House and demanded to see his daughter. The young woman came into the room.

"What can I do for you?" she asked calmly.

"You have been identified as 'F,' the famous Southern spy," said the officer, "and I have come here for the purpose of taking you into custody."

She submitted without a murmur and with a smile. Evidently she knew the danger of her calling and expected to be arrested at any time. The young woman was searched and in her possession were found a number of letters and papers from Southern officers. Also was found her commission from General Stuart which Miss Clarke had considerately left behind. At the time

Odell was placing "F" under arrest other officers were making a search of her home which was still occupied by members of her family. They found quite a number of damaging papers, and also a large quantity of Confederate money. That same night "F" was taken to Washington and lodged in the old Capital prison.

General Baker, in a report upon the subject which he made to Edwin M. Stanton, the Secretary of War, enclosing this commission, said:

"This document, undoubtedly authentic and bearing the genuine signature and private seal of General J. E. B. Stuart, is of itself strong evidence of the appreciation of which 'F's' treasonable services as a spy and informer were held by her Rebel employers. The proof of 'F's' former employment in the service may be considered indisputable; that of her more recent services and especially in connection with the late attack upon our outpost at Fairfax Court House is not less conclusive; that proof consists in the voluntary acknowledgment and declaration by 'F' that she made herself acquainted while a resident within our lines at Fairfax Court House of all the particulars relating to the numbers of our forces there and in the neighborhood, the location of our camps, the places where officers' quarters were established, the precise points where our pickets were stationed, the strength of the outposts, the names of officers in command, the nature of general orders and all other information valuable to the Rebel leaders; that such information had been communicated by her to Captain Mosby of the Confederate Army immediately before the attack on our outposts above mentioned; and that it has been in consequence of the precision and correctness of such information that Captain Mosby had been enabled successfully to attack and surprise the pickets and outposts of our forces, to find without delay or difficulty the quarters of General Stoughton and other United States officers, to capture that officer and a large amount of Government property and effect a large return within the Confederate lines.

"'F' also stated to my informant that Captain Mosby had, but a short time before the rebel raid at Fairfax, been a guest at 'F's' house at that place, that he had remained there three days and three nights, disguised in citizen's dress and that during such visit she had given to him all the information and details which afterward enabled him successfully to attack our forces. 'F' also stated that on an occasion while she was taking a ride on horseback, accompanied by a member of General Stoughton's staff, they were met by Captain Mosby, also on horseback, but in citizen's dress and that she and Captain Mosby recognized and saluted each other."

The official histories of the Civil War are singularly silent regarding the fate of the celebrated "F." Was she tried and convicted? Or was she acquitted and released? Her identity was proven, but it is not written in the records of the war, and consequently it is not given in this narrative. It is known that President Lincoln, with his shrewd, common sense, and his wonderful ability to make the best of perplexing situations, did not look upon the girl as a dreadful offender. But if he was not willing to condemn her, he was not disposed to formally condone her offense. What happened to her? Can it be possible that the door of her cell was conveniently left open one night, and that on the following morning she was not found in her accustomed place? Quite likely. At all events the reader is free to draw any conclusion he, or she, may like.

One thing certain is that she did return to her home in Virginia, and that her descendants are to-day among the residents of the Old Dominion.

10

The mysterious man who asked for the light

One afternoon in the summer of 1898, a shrewd, bright-eyed looking man stepped up to another man in a corridor of a hotel in Toronto, Canada, and asked him if he would give him a light for his cigarette.

A trivial incident, one might say, and yet upon that insignificant episode rested a movement which had for its object the ridding of the United States of Spanish spies in the war which was then going on between this country and the Kingdom of Spain.

In order to make this veracious record perfectly clear it is necessary to retrace our steps. For many months prior to the time mentioned, the relations between the United States and Spain had been greatly strained because of the troublesome Cuban situation. President McKinley had entered a serious protest to the King of Spain, and told him that it was important for our peace that the Cubans should be pacified. But they were not pacified, and things went on from bad to worse until they came to a startling and dramatic climax on the fifteenth of February, 1898, when the cruiser Maine was blown up in the harbor of Havana and a number of Americans were killed.

A wave of indignation swept the country from Maine to California. A chorus went up from all classes in favor of demanding satisfaction from Spain – for, in the popular mind, Spain was responsible for the outrage. The cry everywhere was "Remember the Maine!" Prior to that time the Spanish Minister had been recalled from Washington because of an indiscretion, and now our Minister at Madrid, General Woodford, was handed his passports, and on April 22, President McKinley issued a proclamation saying that a state of war existed between this nation and Spain.

That is history and is known to all. What followed is likewise history, but it is by no means so well known. The first act of the State Department was to inform all of the members of the staff of the Spanish Embassy – in polite language, of course – that their room was preferable to their company. This seemed like a matter of form that did not deserve much thought. And the State Department, having served the required notice, promptly forgot it. But there was one bureau of the United States Government where it was kept in mind, and that was the Secret Service Division.

JOHN E. WILKIE

John E. Wilkie was then the Chief of that most important branch of the Treasury Department, and he had been voted a modest sum by Congress for the purpose of keeping the country free from spies. Heretofore his work had been to keep the nation free from counterfeiters. In both cases he was dealing with crafty and elusive enemies. He proceeded to build up a war organization and he posted his best men in the large cities of this country and Canada. In his office he had a large map of the United States, and by the use of steel pins he could tell at a glance just where his operatives were located. Thus he had men acting as the eyes and the ears of the Government in the cities of Montreal, Toronto, New York, Philadelphia, Washington, Newport News, Savannah, Jacksonville, Tampa, Key West, Mobile, New Orleans, Galveston and San Francisco.

Now, when the members of the staff of the Spanish Embassy were told to get out of the country Wilkie determined to make it his business to see that they did get out. To make sure, he furnished them with an escort – an invisible escort – in the person of the operatives of the Secret Service Division. He suspected that some of them would be so interested in the game of war that they might be tempted to remain on this side of the ocean and take part in the game. And his suspicions were perfectly correct. For instance, Ramon Carranza, who had been Naval Attaché at Washington, found it convenient to linger in the city of Toronto. That would have been perfectly proper if he had not been found talking to a person who was far from proper.

And this is where this story really begins – with the episode of the man who asked for a light in the semi-darkened corridor of a Toronto hotel. The operative who had been sent to the Canadian city by Chief Wilkie happened to stop at the same hotel as the former Attaché of the Spanish Embassy. By a curious coincidence he happened to get a room directly adjoining the one occupied by Señor Carranza. And, moreover, he happened to see every one that came in or out of that room. Also, he overheard some of the conversation that went on in the apartment. Thus on the afternoon with which we are concerned he saw a man with a hang-dog look go into the room, and from time to time he caught fragments of conversation. One of the things he heard the Visitor say was "so I will write to the address you have given me in Montreal." There was some further talk, which could only be heard indistinctly, but the listener managed to discover that the man who was doing the talking had a surprising knowledge of the conditions at the Brooklyn Navy Yard. Presently the conversation came to an end and the visitor left the room. The listener left his room at the same moment, and he came into contact with the other man in the hallway. As they gained the head of the stairway he turned to the strange talker in the most casual manner and said:

"I beg your pardon, but will you kindly favor me with a light for my cigarette?"

The mysterious stranger halted and courteously complied with the request. And in those few seconds in that dim hallway, by the light of the burning match, the Secret Service operative obtained what he most desired – a view of the other man's face. In that brief period of time the characteristics of the suspect were indelibly stamped upon his memory. The two men parted. The one who had been closeted with the former Naval Attaché of the Spanish Embassy went out into the street and proceeded to a remote part of the city. He went to an obscure hotel and registered and was given a room. The operative of the Secret Service followed him and at the first convenient opportunity he scrutinized the hotel register. The name he found inscribed thereon was "Alexander Cree." His theory was that it was an assumed name. At all events he shadowed his man. He watched his every movement, and soon afterwards he sent a code telegram to John E. Wilkie, the Chief of the Secret Service at Washington.

The scene now shifts to the National Capital. Mr. Wilkie was still in his office occupied with the duties which pressed heavily upon a man in charge of an important department, and whose force was scarcely large enough for the work they were called upon to do day by day at a most critical stage in the history of the nation. Shortly before midnight the telegram came from Toronto. It was given to the code man of the office and in a short time he had transcribed it. In plain English it read as follows:

"Young Southerner, Alexander Cree, of Hillsboro, I think, leaves for Washington to-night. My height and build, small, dark moustache, black soft felt hat, black sack coat, black sailor tie, somewhat shabby, evidently served on Brooklyn, has intimate knowledge of Naval matters. Just had long interview with Naval Attaché. He is to write to Montreal."

This was news with a vengeance. There was great activity about the offices of the Secret Service Division that night. Several of the best men who were in the city were quickly summoned and given a description of the man who was expected from Canada. It was almost midnight when Chief Wilkie left for his home, but when he quit the Department to get a few hours' sleep it was with the knowledge that he had made arrangements for giving Mr. Cree a hospitable reception upon his arrival in Washington.

That night every railroad station leading into the Capital was closely guarded by Secret Service men. They carefully scrutinized every passenger who alighted, paying special attention to those who were likely to have come from Canada. It was a big job, but it was performed with thoroughness. Many a passenger that night must have been annoyed at the manner in which he was watched by the alert representatives of the United States Government. But, if they felt any annoyance, they must have realized that they were living in war times and must expect all sorts of queer things. Finally, "Mr. Alexander Cree" arrived, and it is significant of the efficiency of the system that he was immediately spotted by the waiting detectives. The description sent by the operative at Toronto had served them well. They recognized him as easily as if they were in possession of his photograph.

From that moment there was a Secret Service man watching him. When one man was tired another quickly took his place, and, as a consequence, there was not a thing he did, and scarcely a thing he said, that was not known to Chief Wilkie a few hours afterwards. His first move was to get something to eat, which was an entirely natural and by no means an unpatriotic act. But after that he went to the Navy Department, and apparently wandered about in an aimless manner. But, as a matter of fact, he had a purpose in visiting that place. Just whether someone in the Department was acting in collusion with him was not clearly established. Finally he went to his lodgings on E Street. He occupied a second-story room, and as soon as he reached it he made a light and settled down to work before a desk which could be seen from the street. Evidently a quantity of mail had accumulated during his absence in the Dominion, because he was occupied for some time in opening and reading letters. For hours he remained there silhouetted against the window shade while the Secret Service men on the opposite side of the street observed every move he made.

Thus, while Washington slept, an enemy of the Republic and its defenders engaged in a game that was to have the greatest bearing upon the conduct of the war. It is difficult to decide which was the most amazing, the daring and impudence of the conspirator in thus working under the very dome of the Capitol, or the pertinacity and bull-dog determination of the Secret Service operatives in keeping this man under their constant supervision. It began to look as if he would never go to bed. But presently there was a movement in the room and in a few minutes the dark-complexioned man in the soft hat came out of the house and walked across the street in the direction of a letter box. He opened the lid and slid a long envelope into the aperture. Then he turned and went back to his lodgings. In a little while the light was extinguished300 and then "Alexander Cree" retired to sleep the sleep – if not of the just at least of the industrious man.

But the Secret Service operatives did not go to sleep. They were more alert than ever. One man kept guard over the lodgings of the suspect and the other remained by the side of the letter box. At daylight he got into communication with Chief Wilkie, and as a consequence of his report an arrangement was made with the Postmaster of Washington by which that particular letter box was opened, and the particular missive dropped into the box by the man from Toronto turned over to Chief Wilkie. A short time later a "council of war" was held in the office of the Chief of the Secret Service. The object of interest was the suspected letter. It was in an ordinary white, oblong envelope, and it was addressed to F. W. Dicken, 1248 Dorchester Street, Montreal, Canada. The address instantly called to mind the report of the operative in Toronto. He had heard the mysterious stranger say to the Naval Attaché "so I am to write to the address you have given me in Montreal." It was evident that they were "getting warm" as the children say in their games. But when the letter was opened all need for conjecture was past. The amazing communication read as follows:

"A cipher message has been sent from the Navy Department to San Francisco directing the Cruiser Charleston to proceed to Manila with 500 men and machinery for repairs to Dewey. A long cipher has been received from Dewey at Department at 3.30301 o'clock. They are translating it now. Cannot find it out yet. Have heard important news respecting movements of colliers and cruisers. Newark at Norfolk Navy Yard; also about the new Holland boat, as to what they intend to do with her and her destination, I shall go to Norfolk soon to find important news. My address will be Norfolk House, Norfolk, Virginia, but shall not go until Tuesday."

This was signed "G. D." and was marked "in haste." The first move of Chief Wilkie was to make sure that the man was guarded. His investigations proved that there was no possibility of "G. D."

escaping from Washington. Then he got into communication with the Secretary of War and the Secretary of the Navy and informed them of the information that had been intercepted. The immediate effect of this was to tighten the discipline in each of these Departments. All unauthorized persons were to be kept out of the building and a strict watch was kept upon all of the employees. The inference was that someone in the Navy Department had been co-operating with "G. D." and that this person had supplied him with information upon his return from Canada.

The question of taking the spy into custody was next considered. It was decided that this should be done at once. As it was a matter that technically came under the military power of the Government, Chief Wilkie made application to the War Department, and as a result of this Captain Saye of the Eighth Artillery, with a corporal and one other man, was ordered to report to him for duty. Thus fortified, the head of the Secret Service Division started for the apartment on E Street. The little procession going from the Treasury Department attracted very little attention, and the passers-by did not realize what was going on. But all of those in the little group understood the importance of their mission so far as the Government was concerned.

It was eleven o'clock at night and when they arrived at the house occupied by "G. D." they discovered a light burning in the second-story room. It was evident that the spy was continuing his habits of industry. The Chief gained admission without any difficulty, and, followed by the others, made for the upper room. The supposed Alexander Cree was sitting at his desk engaged in writing. He seemed surprised at the intrusion, but received his callers politely. Evidently his calling had accustomed him to visits at all hours of the day and night.

"Well, gentlemen," he said, "what can I do for you?"

"To start with," said the spokesman of the invading party, "we would like to have the letter you are writing and all of the documents you have in that desk."

For the first time he showed surprise. He smiled faintly and then rejoined:

"Perhaps you will let me know the cause of this unexpected visit."

"Certainly. We have come to arrest you as a spy!"

Cree turned very white. He steadied himself by resting against the side of a bureau. It was some moments before he was able to speak, and then moistening his lips with the tip of his tongue he murmured:

"Who are you, and what authority have you got for talking in this manner?"

"It's no use, young man," was the quick retort, "we have the goods on you, and if you have any doubt about it we can show you the letter which you mailed to Montreal and which has been intercepted by the United States Government."

The spy looked at the speaker helplessly. His white face contrasted sharply with his black moustache. For a moment he swayed uncertainly, and fell to the floor in a heap. He was a most abject spectacle, and it was necessary to carry him out of the room. That night he spent in a cell, facing a charge of treason against the Government, and wondering what his fate would be.

A mass of compromising letters and papers were found in the room. From some of these it was proven that "G. D." was a naturalized citizen and a former yeoman on the cruiser Brooklyn. What had prompted him to turn against his own country? Could it have been some grievance, real or fancied? Was it Spanish gold? Chief Wilkie discovered many interesting things among the papers that were found in the room on E Street. Among them was a slip of paper which contained what is known as Slater's Code. It said: "To send add 100; to receive subtract 100." This was the key to the cipher which he was to employ in sending messages to his employers. The cipher contained thousands of ordinary words arranged alphabetically and having fixed consecutive numbers of five figures each. Why he had not employed it in the compromising communication to Montreal was never known. Possibly over-confidence had made him careless for the moment.

In the meantime Chief Wilkie had his organization working overtime. The United States map in his office containing the little steel pins to indicate the position of his men in different parts of the United States and Canada was consulted repeatedly during the next twenty-four hours. Telegrams in code were sent in all directions. As the result another spy was captured in Tampa, Florida. By one of the curious freaks of fate this man was critically ill when he was taken into custody and died shortly afterwards. But the greatest activity was in Canada. It was learned that the Dorchester Street house had only been leased a few days before, and that it was intended as the rendezvous of the Spanish spies in Canada. It was clear that a private detective agency had been organized in Canada for the purpose of obtaining information concerning the movements of the American troops.

Another amazing thing that was discovered in connection with this spy system related to the manner in which these men were to work. They were to join the United States army and to go with the army of invasion into Cuba, Porto Rico and the Philippines. When the opportunity offered they were to permit themselves to be captured by the Spanish soldiers. After furnishing all of the information possible to the enemy they were to return to the American lines and continue their system of espionage. All of this was worked out with the greatest attention to detail. Each one of the spies was supplied with a plain gold or silver ring. On this was engraved the words "Confienza Augustine." That was to be their means of identification to the Spanish Generals. Needless to say, the discovery of the plot nipped that scheme in the bud, and rendered it useless for the remainder of the war.

But what Chief Wilkie and his associates desired more than anything else was some evidence to directly connect the members of the late Spanish Embassy with the operations of "G. D." and the plot in Canada. It came sooner than was expected. One of the Secret Service operatives who investigated the Dorchester Street house found some letters which established this connection. One of them was a communication from Ramon Carranza to Señor Don Jose Gomez Ymas. It was short and sweet. It said: "We have had bad luck for they have captured two of our best spies – one in Washington and the other in Tampa."

This made it appear that the former Naval Attaché was quite as indiscreet as the supposed Alexander Cree. At all events, the evidence in the case was furnished to Lord Pauncefoote, the English Ambassador to Washington, and, upon his representations, the Canadian authorities made it their business to deport the entire Spanish outfit.

Two days later the Chief of the Secret Service Division went to the jail at the National Capital for the purpose of interviewing the man who had permitted himself to be made a dupe of the Spanish Government. When the door of the cell was opened a dreadful sight met his eyes:

"G. D.," the chief spy of the Spanish-American war, had hanged himself – a dramatic and horrible climax to one of the most interesting incidents in American history.

11

The romantic side of Major Andre's unsuccessful exploits

All the world loves a lover, and the fact that the unfortunate Major John André was engaged to be married to a charming English girl at the time of his execution helped to place him in something like a romantic light before the world. He had another advantage. The blackness of the treason of Benedict Arnold made André shine by comparison, so that while the American was regarded with horror and contempt everywhere, the unhappy fate of the young Englishman excited universal sympathy.

It was in 1769 that André met Miss Honora Sneyd in Litchfield, England. It was a case of love at first sight, ardent and impetuous on both sides. But, alas, as is usual, the course of true love did not run smoothly. The match was disapproved by Miss Sneyd's father, and the young man was told to keep away from the house of his adored one. To make assurance doubly sure he was sent to his father's counting house in London. He tried hard to accustom himself to office drudgery, but in spite of his best intentions the face of Honora kept popping up from amidst the rows of figures, and upsetting his calculations.

His was an adventurous spirit, and in 1771 he tossed aside his ledgers and day books to accept a commission in a regiment bound for America. There was an affecting scene when he parted from Miss Sneyd and she gave him her portrait as a souvenir. He plighted his troth anew and promised that the picture should never part from him under any circumstances – a promise that was kept with pathetic fidelity.

Before he had been in America long André, by reason of his courage and intelligence, rose to the position of aide-de-camp to Sir Henry Clinton, commander-in-chief of the British forces. It was at this juncture that Benedict Arnold, smarting under supposed wrongs, made a proposition to the British to betray to them the post at West Point, of which he was in command. It was regarded as the key to the American position and General Clinton designated Major André as the man to conduct the negotiations with the traitor Arnold. The importance of this position was equalled by its danger.

The conspiracy between Arnold and André had been carried on by means of correspondence for quite a while. They wrote under fictitious names, and naturally the greatest secrecy was observed. But finally the time came when it was necessary to hold a personal meeting in order to bring the treason to a head. Major André at that time held the position of adjutant general in the British army, and it was at Arnold's request that he was detailed to meet the traitorous general for the purpose of settling all the details. On the 20th of September, 1780, André went on board the British sloop of war *Vulture* with Colonel Beverly Robinson, and proceeded up the Hudson with a view of holding an interview with Arnold. There is a strong feeling, or at least circumstantial evidence, which indicates that Robinson was partially responsible for bringing Arnold to the state of mind where he was willing to sacrifice his country in order to satisfy his own wounded vanity. At all events, they made the trip together and on the night of the 21st a boat was sent by Arnold to the *Vulture* which brought André to the shore about six miles below Stony Point.

In a secluded spot and after midnight the conspirators met and prepared the plans by which the American cause was to be betrayed. Daylight appeared and still the conference went on. It was suggested that it would be desirable to have breakfast, and at Arnold's invitation André consented to accompany him to the house of Joshua Smith, which was about two miles below the meeting place. They sat there for a long time and presently the booming of cannon was heard and they saw that the *Vulture* had weighed anchor and was proceeding down the river. This was due to the fact that Colonel Livingston of the American army thought that she was too near the American outposts, and with characteristic promptness he brought cannon to bear on the vessel and compelled her to descend the river.

This interfered seriously with the scheme that had been agreed upon between the Englishman and the American. Plans of the American works, their armament, the number of troops they contained and other important details were handed by Arnold to André. To make sure that he should not lose the precious papers Major André took off his boots and placed the documents between his stockings and his feet. As it was evident that André would not be able to reach the *Vulture* Arnold furnished him with a horse and gave him a pass which directed the guards to permit him to go where he pleased on the ground that he was engaged in public business. A similar pass was given to Joshua Smith who had acted as host to the spy and the traitor. Major André passed the entire day at Smith's house in the hope and expectation of being able to get aboard the *Vulture* at night, but when evening arrived Smith became frightened and declined to row out to the *Vulture*. He proposed instead to cross the river with André and then see that he was put on the road by which he might return to New York. The Englishman was greatly disappointed, but was finally induced to throw Smith's overcoat over his uniform, and shortly before dusk they started to go across at Kings Ferry. They succeeded in making about eight miles on the other side when they were stopped by an American sentinel. Arnold's pass satisfied the officer in command but he warned them against proceeding any farther at night.

THE MEETING BETWEEN BENEDICT ARNOLD AND MAJOR ANDRÉ

They remained at a farmhouse until morning and by that time had now approached a portion of the country some thirty miles in extent which lay between the lines of the opposing armies and was considered neutral ground. After proceeding three miles farther toward New York André and his host breakfasted at a farmhouse and then parted. Smith returned home and André continued on his way to New York, confident that he was past all danger and that it was only a question of time when the treason of Arnold would be completed.

He was going through a wooded glen when he was suddenly confronted by three men, the first of whom was clothed in a manner which might suggest his connection with the British army.

"Good morning," exclaimed André, imprudently. "Gentlemen, I hope you belong to our party."

"What party?" asked the leader of the trio.

"The lower party," said André, indicating the camp of the British army.

"We do," said the leader, but with a significant look at his companions.

The young Englishman was now entirely off his guard and declared himself to be a British officer. He said that he had been up the country on most important business and must not be detained on any account. He drew out his gold watch as evidence of his statement, but to his surprise, the foremost of the young men clutched him by the shoulder and exclaimed:

"You are our prisoner!"

It afterwards became known that the three men were farmers of the neighborhood, their names being John Paulding, Isaac Van Wort and David Williams. Paulding happened by chance to be wearing an overcoat that had been left on his place by a British soldier, and it was this uniform that had misled André.

The English major was very much exercised by this time and now remembered his pass. He exhibited the paper that had been given to him by General Arnold, saying:

"You see that I am all right. This pass permits me to go through the lines."

Paulding, however, was convinced that there was something wrong. He seized the bridle of André's horse and compelled him to dismount and then subjected him to a very close search. They took off his boots and his stockings and found the concealed papers. Paulding read them carefully and as he came across the incriminating words exclaimed:

"My God, he is a spy!"

The Englishman used all of his persuasive powers on his captors, but in vain. He offered them any amount of money if they would release him, but they refused and conducted their prisoner to Lieutenant Colonel Jameson, who was in command of the post at New Castle. He in turn instantly sent the papers found in André's possession by express to General Washington, who was then returning from a visit to the French at Hartford.

By a curious chain of circumstances Washington was returning with the members of his own military family, including General Lafayette and General Knox. On the morning of the 25th of September he sent a messenger to General Arnold saying that the party would breakfast with him on that day. As they approached Arnold's headquarters at the Robinson house Washington turned aside from the direct route in order to visit the defences on the east side of the Hudson. Lafayette, with the proverbial politeness of the French, suggested that Mrs. Arnold would be waiting breakfast for them.

"Ah," replied Washington, "you young men are all in love with Mrs. Arnold. I see that you are eager to be with her as soon as possible. Go and breakfast with her and tell her not to wait for me. I must ride down and examine the redoubts on this side of the river. I will be with you shortly."

His request was complied with. Lafayette and his friends found Mrs. Arnold – who was the famous Peggy Shippen – as usual, bright, gay and fascinating. Arnold himself was strangely grave and thoughtful. In the very midst of the breakfast a horseman galloped to the door and gave a letter to Arnold, which stated that André was a prisoner and that the papers found in his boots had been forwarded to General Washington. Arnold was compelled to act quickly in this crisis and he gave remarkable evidence of quickness of mind.

"Gentlemen," he said to his guests, "I am compelled to leave you for a time and hope that I may be excused."

From the breakfast room he hurried to Mrs. Arnold's apartments, and when she came to him in response to his summons explained his position, saying: "I must fly instantly. My life depends on my reaching the British lines without detection."

It was perhaps a few hours after this that the letters and papers which told the story of Arnold's perfidy were handed to Washington. Washington read them calmly and, calling Lafayette and Knox, told them the story, adding sadly:

"Who can we trust now?"

Hot on the heels of this came one from Major André explaining his position and saying that he had been betrayed into the vile condition of an enemy in disguise within the American posts. He asked that in any rigor policy might dictate he should not be branded with anything dishonorable, as he considered himself a messenger in the service of the king and not an involuntary impostor. He said that he wrote to vindicate his fame and not to solicit security. To this letter Washington made no reply.

On the 26th of September Major Tallmadge, having André in custody, arrived at the Robinson house. General Washington declined to see the prisoner but gave orders that he should be treated with every courtesy and civility consistent with his absolute security.

The charming personality of the prisoner won for him the personal regard of all with whom he was brought into contact. His immediate jailor said that it often drew tears from his eyes to find André so agreeable in conversation on different subjects while he – the American officer – was reflecting on the future fate of the young Englishman.

While Tallmadge was on the way with André to the American headquarters their conversation became very frank and their relations friendly. Presently André asked Tallmadge with what light he would be regarded by General Washington at a military tribunal. The American hesitated, but when André repeated the question he said:

"I had a much loved chum in Yale College by the name of Nathan Hale, who entered the army in 1775. Immediately before the battle of Long Island General Washington wanted information respecting the strength, position and probable movements of the enemy. Captain Hale volunteered his services, went over to Brooklyn and was taken just as he was passing the outposts of the enemy on his return. Do you remember the sequel of the story?"

"Yes," said André, in a low voice that was tremulous with emotion. "He was hanged as a spy. But you surely do not consider his case and mine alike."

"Yes, precisely similar," said Major Tallmadge, "and your fate will be a similar one."

Washington in the meantime had received a number of communications from General Clinton concerning the case of Major André. Clinton, Arnold and Robinson conferred together as to the means of obtaining the release of André. Arnold wrote a letter to Clinton assuming the responsibility for André's conduct, declaring that he came to him under the protection of a flag of truce, and that he gave him passports to go to White Plains on his return to New York. This impertinent letter from the traitor, enclosed in one from himself, Clinton forwarded to Washington, claiming that André should be permitted to return to New York.

As might be expected, these letters had no influence upon the action of Washington. He referred the case of the prisoner to a board of general officers, which he ordered to meet on the 29th of September, 1780, and directed that after a careful examination this board should report their opinion "of the light in which Major André should be considered and the punishment that ought to be inflicted." This board consisted of six major generals and eight brigadier generals, who went into the case with unusual care.

When Major André was brought before the board of officers he met with every indulgence, and was requested to answer no questions which would even embarrass his feelings. He frankly confessed all the facts relating to himself. Indeed, the facts were not controverted, and the board reported that André ought to be considered as a spy, and, agreeable to the usages of nations, must suffer death. André met the result with manly firmness.

"I foresaw my fate," said he, "and though I do not pretend to play the hero or to be indifferent about life, yet I am reconciled to whatever may happen, conscious that misfortune and not guilt has brought it upon me."

The execution was to have taken place on the 1st of October at five o'clock in the evening, but Washington received a second letter from Clinton expressing the opinion that the board had not been rightly informed of all the circumstances on which a judgment ought to be formed and adding, "I think it of the highest moment to humanity that your Excellency should be perfectly appraised of the state of this matter before you proceed to put that judgment into execution."

Accordingly he sent three of his staff officers to give Washington, as he declared, the true state of the facts. These gentlemen came accompanied by Colonel Beverly Robinson. General Greene on the part of Washington met the party and after a long conference left to report to Washington all that had been urged in behalf of André. Later General Greene sent a note to Colonel Robinson informing him that he had made as full a report of their conference as his memory would permit, but that it had made no alteration in the opinion and determination of Washington.

André died possessing the sympathy of his judges and the friendship of all the American officers with whom he had been brought into familiar intercourse. Both Tallmadge and Hamilton expressed for him an attachment almost passionate. He died in the full uniform of his rank in the British army. A letter from André to Sir Henry Clinton expressed gratitude for his kindness and commended to his consideration his mother and sister and excusing his commander from all responsibility for his fate, saying among other things, "I have obtained General Washington's permission to send you this letter, the object of which is to remove from your breast any suspicion that I should imagine that I was bound by your Excellency's orders to expose myself to what has happened. The events of coming within an enemy's lines and of changing my dress, which led me to my present situation, were contrary to my own intentions as they were to your orders, and the circuitous route upon which I took to return was pressed, perhaps unavoidably and without alternative, upon me. I am perfectly tranquil in mind and prepared for any fate to which an honest zeal for my king's service may have conducted me."

On the 10th of August, 1821, the remains of André were removed from the banks of the Hudson to Westminster Abbey and interred there near the monument which had long been erected to his memory. In the south aisle near the window and surrounded by many great names is his monument on which is inscribed:

"Sacred to the memory of Major John André, who rose by his merits at an early period of life to the rank of Adjutant-General of the British forces in America; and employed in an important but hazardous enterprise, fell a sacrifice to his zeal for his king and country, on the Second of October, 1780. Age 29. Universally beloved and esteemed by the army in which he served and lamented even by his foes.

"His Grace and Sovereign, King George III, has caused this monument to be erected."

It is an interesting fact that André never ceased in his affection for Honora Sneyd. He kept his pledge to be faithful to her always. His letters are full of the hopes and expectations of ambitious young manhood. While in New York with Sir Henry Clinton he was a great social favorite. Many proud young women, especially among the Tories, would have been glad of a matrimonial alliance with the handsome young aide-de-camp. André was human enough to appreciate and enjoy all of this flattery, but his heart was true to the girl he met in Litchfield. When the three farmers arrested him they stripped him – as they thought – of all he possessed, but he managed to keep the portrait of Miss Sneyd, which he always carried about his person, by concealing it in his mouth. He thought of her to the last.

And the pathos of it all lay in the fact that he expired in ignorance of the fact that she had died in London, two months before.

www.ingramcontent.com/pod-product-compliance
Ingram Content Group UK Ltd.
Pitfield, Milton Keynes, MK11 3LW, UK
UKHW040004200726
13854UKWH00001B/27